MW00915893

OMG, THAT'S ME! 3

Bipolar Disorder, Depression, PTSD,
Mental Health and Humor

DAVE MOWRY AND TARA ROLSTAD

Published by Vandever Publishing, Portland Oregon.

ISBN: 9798713505158

Dedicated to our families—especially Dave's wife, Heather, and Tara's husband, David—and to all those struggling with mental health who face each day with courage and humor.

ACKNOWLEDGMENTS

We are grateful to bring readers this second edition of our book, now joining the *"OMG, That's Me"* series. This book is about the power of humor to reshape our perspectives and our experiences. Without humor, our comedy journeys would never have happened. Dave's life would still be sad. Tara would still be a victim of her family members' chaos. The stories of the amazing comics in this book would not be told.

Speaking of those amazing comics, we must thank Lorayne, Martin, Eric and Molly for letting us tell their stories. You are strong, funny, courageous comedians and advocates, and we know lives will be changed because you were willing to let us include you in these pages. We continue to owe you a tremendous debt of gratitude, and maybe some cookies.

The first edition of our book was made possible by many, including Stand Up for Mental Health founder David Granirer; the National Alliance on Mental Illness in Clackamas

County, Oregon; and the generous contributions of Tom and Carol Baker, Jeff Caton and more than 70 different supporters of our original Kickstarter campaign. We are grateful for their trust and their support. We are also grateful for our original editor, Leanne Sype, who believed in us as authors, and in the importance of these stories.

TABLE OF CONTENTS

INTRODUCTION

Mental illness can be dark, scary, and depressing, and most people think they would rather get an enema than hang out with a bunch of mentally ill people. We get it, that's what we used to think too, until we WERE those people, or loved those people! Here, we share our stories of how humor—performing stand-up comedy about mental health, of all things—has changed our lives. We hope you find this book funny, poignant, and serious all at the same time, and you never think of bipolar disorder, schizophrenia, autism, PTSD or depression the same way again.

Some might think we, Dave and Tara, are making fun of ourselves, but that's not it. We became friends through a program called Stand Up for Mental Health (SMH), where we learned to share our stories of hospital stays, taking medications, doctor's visits and more. We've discovered that when we seek out and find humor in our stories, and when we joke about the absurd and the aggravating, it gives us power over those difficult experiences. We are no longer victims of our disorders or our circumstances.

We've learned to share through humor and comedy what we never felt we could share in normal conversation. By talking openly about mental health, and by performing our acts, we break through society's barriers of stigma and shame. Once you get past our diagnoses you will see mental illness like you have never seen it before, and you'll see that we are able, intelligent, and funny people.

Even if you are not aware of it, you probably know someone with a mental illness. One adult in five will experience mental illness in any given year, according to the National Alliance on Mental Illness. It isn't just grown-ups, either, as one in five teenagers also experiences mental illness.

In this book we want to gently confront your preconceived notions and your prejudices:

- *Think everyone with mental illness got there because of drug and alcohol use?*
- *Think people with mental illness who are on disability are living large on the government?*
- *Think people who are depressed should just try harder, pray more, exercise or take vitamins?*
- *Think that being diagnosed with severe mental illness means a lifetime of psych units or homelessness?*

If you answered yes to any of those questions, think again.

You will find aspects of yourself reflected in these pages. You will find elements that remind you of loved ones, friends, and coworkers. But most importantly you will find the stories of amazing people whose experiences of mental illness have been transformed through the perspective of humor and stand-up comedy.

From Dave: I first learned comedy from Stand Up for Mental Health classes in Clackamas County, and invited Tara to join our group for our first performance. Soon after, Tara and I started facilitating and teaching comedy classes. It has been such a powerful experience that we decided we needed to share the stories of some of our comics with the world.

In this book, we share the stories of just a few of the people who have gone through our classes. These special people are brave, inspiring, and funny. We feel fortunate to know them and to have seen their transformations; it is an honor to share their stories and our own with you.

Our goal is changing minds and hearts, allowing readers to see people differently, and showing that people with a mental illness are so much more than our diagnosis. We can be whole and funny and hopeful.

Dave Mowry

From Tara: Society seems to approach mental health, and mental illness, in one of two prevailing ways. First, thankfully, there is a growing familiarity and comfort with garden variety mental health issues such as depression or anxiety *(as if there was such a thing as garden variety depression or anxiety)*. These issues are getting much easier to admit to, to talk about, and to feel comfortable getting treatment. I am always amazed by how many moms in whatever group or circle I am in will easily admit that they are or have been on antidepressants *(especially after a glass of wine!)* We compare prescriptions as easily as if we were comparing recipes or vacation plans.

The second and still too prevalent view is one that lumps together all other severe mental illness into one bucket. Should you or someone you love wind up in that bucket, society assumes life as you knew it is over. It is further assumed that you or your family member will live a low-functioning life, sad and tragic. End of story.

Mental illness myth: *People with severe mental illness are doomed to be "sick" their whole lives.*

Truth: Recovery from mental illness is possible, *even severe mental illness, with the right treatments, access to care and therapies and providers, and time. Recovery might not look the same as life without mental illness, but meaningful, productive life is possible.*

Working in mental health comedy, as well as our association with the National Alliance on Mental Illness, has given Dave and I hope that recovery can occur even for the most severe cases and diagnoses, because we've seen it happen.

If I have that hope, I can hold onto it for my nieces in their worst moments when they can't hope for themselves. Without that hope, I wring my hands, pat them on the back, and say "there, there, I guess this is your life now, I'm sorry."

If Dave has that hope, he can hold on to it the next time his bipolar disorder flares, confident in the knowledge that just as he's gotten better before, he can get better again.

We look at hard times through a different lens now, a lens of perspective and humor. Tough stuff happens. Now, we're looking for the funny, which in turns propels us toward hope and healing.

We hope you'll see in these pages that the hope of recovery from mental illness is real. If you live with mental illness, keep fighting for recovery, and work to view others through that same hopeful lens. If you are a friend or family member whose loved one lives with mental illness, hang onto that hope for them. They need you to hope for them and never give up, even when they can't find the strength to hope for themselves.

If all of us begin to share that hope in recovery—people living with mental illness, family members and eventually society—it will change what we expect and demand in terms of treatment, research, and public policy.

Sure, maybe a life in recovery for you or your family member won't look like what you planned, but life can be meaningful and joyful and FUNNY.

Tara Rolstad

Comedy: Funny and Art

Art is serious, sophisticated, high culture; so how in the world can we claim comedy is art?

Every art form derives its power from the ability to evoke emotion, and comedy is an art form. It took a while for us to really understand that, because, well, comedy is fun.

But comedy uses words to shape and then share emotion, whether frustration, anger, confusion, joy, or love, and then serves up that emotion with a surprising twist. It is an act of intricate, sophisticated, emotional word artistry. It is, unquestionably, art that can have tremendous healing power for both artist and audience.

The healing power in the moment a comic realizes that they have rewritten their own story by choosing to find humor in the darkest experiences of their lives is simply transformational. It is a transformation that changes the way we can approach even the hardest moments, looking immediately for the humor, the ridiculous, the punch line that someday will be.

The transformation isn't limited just to the comics, either. Each of our mental health comedy performances is a powerful exercise in not judging people by their appearance, by how they talk, or by their diagnosis. Each show is a stigma buster. Each show is another step in the transformation for both comedian and audience.

Our comics

Many comics we work with start with no particular perception of themselves as funny. They definitely earn a huge gold star.

Showing up to a comedy class when you don't think you are funny AND you are struggling with mental health—that's brave.

Conversely, some new comics come to class having long thought of themselves as funny and having been told by friends and family that they are funny. We've learned that the things that make a person funny in conversation do not automatically translate into being good at stand-up comedy, which can make for an awkward reckoning when they begin the class….

In fact, those who do already think they are funny often have the more difficult time, as they discover that being a smart-crackin' wiseacre does not a comic make. *(Writing "smart-crackin' wiseacre" does, however, make us sound 90 years old.)* It can be a shocking, rude awakening.

Friends and family are often more nervous than the comics at the first performance. More than a few family members have told us that afterward they had only the vaguest awareness or memory of the other comics because they were so focused on their own anxiety, watching their loved one step out into the vulnerability that is the stage. It's particularly hard when they have witnessed a family member's difficult prior public interactions or experiences or have heard the painful details, especially if their loved one has been the victim of stigma, discrimination, or bullying.

They fear what the comics fear, what we feared our first times. *(And our 2nd, 5th, and 14th times, not that we're counting.)* Will anyone laugh? Will it be a real laugh or a pity laugh? Worst of all, will there just be horrible … awkward … silence?

Thankfully, that has never happened to either of us, or any of the students we've worked with. They aren't all equally funny, and their jokes aren't all equally funny, but our experience of these shows is that the audience has already decided to encourage, to cheer, and to clap. They always laugh. Always. Without exception.

We have had the privilege of watching each comic make that scary trip up to the mic, start their act, and realize the power they wield over an audience that has chosen to yield it to them. They share their jokes, they tell their stories, and people laugh.

Dave, who is no longer stuck in his own sadness, who now sees humor where others don't and shares it to make himself and others laugh. Or Tara, who no longer feels trapped by the chaos of her nieces' mental illness but feels empowered to advocate for them and others through humor. You'll love Lorayne, as we do, for her toughness and her no-nonsense stories about six stays in the notorious Oregon State Hospital back in the darker days of mental health treatment. Eric will challenge your prejudices and make you laugh through his journey with schizophrenia. You'll learn from Martin, who lives with autism, charts music scores and tells great jokes. You'll meet Molly McNab, M.D., who was a good doctor until bipolar disorder ended her career and left her feeling like she had nothing to be proud of. Now, she can't stop writing jokes, and she brings down the house!

These six comics are no different, no more or less amazing than any other group of comics we've worked with in our little corner of the Pacific Northwest. Men, women, upper class, middle class, old, young, professional, or blue collar, mental illness doesn't discriminate.

Thankfully, neither does laughter. Laughter releases positive healing chemicals in our body, relaxes our muscles, and lifts our spirits. Laughter is a precious human commodity that grows in the sharing of it, and heck, we're fairly sure it causes weight loss and cures wrinkles. *(No firm data on those last claims, but we're hopeful.)*

CHAPTER 1

DAVE

I live with bipolar disorder and severe anxiety. Which is interesting because the town I live in in Oregon is called "Happy Valley". True, and too funny, right? But the name Happy Valley is really a misnomer... There is no valley. —Dave

Living with bipolar disorder is hard. There is also a significant stigma. The stigma is getting better, but it is still there. When I was first diagnosed with bipolar in my forties, it was bad. When I told people about my mental illness, many disappeared from my life. Friends stopped calling and coming over. My brother and father were in denial. People looked at me differently and talked to me differently. Quickly I learned not to talk about my mental illness. I hid in the shadows and suffered in silence for years. But humor helped me come out of the mental health closet. Humor helped me talk to people about my mental illness. Humor changed my life.

Before comedy: the black hole of depression

I used to be happy and successful. I had a successful business, a nice house, money in the bank, and many friends. But in 1996 I had a breakdown and lost it all. I remember driving between my businesses and feeling under an insurmountable amount of stress and anxiety. My mind was racing with constant negative thoughts. And then my mind just…snapped. I literally heard it. It was like a branch breaking. It was like an electric shock. Like putting my finger in a light socket. My mind went dull. My voice went monotone. The muscles in my face went slack. I tried to gather myself. It was all I could do to get home. I went straight to bed. I stayed in bed for two months.

For those two months it was all I could do to get out of bed to go downstairs and eat. Some days I made it to the couch. I sat there just holding it together. It was everything I could do just to be. Just to exist. There was no peace. Every day I prayed for peace of mind. It didn't come.

Unless you have been under the weight of depression there is no way to know what it is like. The pain is like being slowly crushed under the weight of a collapsing building. Knowing there is life outside of the rubble but not being able to lift the weight to be part of that life. Survival is the only word that fits to describe living in this darkness and pain. I fought to survive.

Now, the slide into darkness has become familiar and oddly comfortable. The pathways in my brain have been well worn. The slow descent starts with a pang of anxiety and a subtle feeling of guilt of something done long ago. Why guilt? I have no idea. Why should something I did twenty years ago come to mind today? What is wrong with my brain that I can remember the smallest angst and yet forget the times of joy? This is what happens with my bipolar illness and severe anxiety disorder. I feel cursed.

The depression grows slowly at first, then the negative thoughts quicken. This can take hours, or it can take days. The light in my eyes grows dim. My face slackens. My voice turns to barely a whisper, and when I talk it is in one-word sentences. I do nothing but sit and try to just be; try to hold it together. I am in the black hole with barely a wisp of light at the top. Part of my brain is trying to get out while another part settles in for a long hibernation. Lost and alone, I suffer in silence.

The sense of loss I feel batters my brain. I go into mourning for the things I have missed in the past 55 years and what I am missing in the present. This adds to the anxiety and depression. I have overwhelming feelings of self-loathing. I am a failure. I am not a good husband, father, or friend. I am unworthy of happiness. I have nothing to offer anyone.

In addition to depression, I've also struggled with anxiety throughout my life. I fought it every day. In the morning I would wake up and it was the first feeling of the day. At night it was the last thing I felt. Between day and night there was fear, apprehension, heartache, and sadness. In some ways the anxiety was the worst of my mental illness because it was always present.

I was insane. I was always stuck inside my head with racing thoughts and feelings of complete self-loathing. The weight of the crushing lows was so great that there was no relief. I wanted so badly to escape the pain. I found temporary relief in drugs and alcohol. But only very temporary. The beast always returned.

Dying somehow felt scary and inviting. Peace of mind. Oh god, peace of mind. How I craved it. Dying would end the suffering. I came close to taking my own life, but I did not pull the trigger. I had driven out to a river about an hour from my house. I sat alone at a picnic table watching the river flow by. With the gun in my lap, I felt calm. Killing myself was my first option. The closer I got to pulling the trigger the more thoughts of my family came into my head. Killing myself would end my pain but it would bring pain, suffering, guilt, and a forever presence to them.

I sat for three hours. I had no concept of time. Only the cool breeze at sunset got my attention. I had lived another three hours. I could make it 24 and then 48 and then days and weeks. My family saved my life. I had something to live for—a reason to fight my demons. Family was one thing that made sense in my insane world.

The depression took its toll on me just as it does with other sufferers. I suffered in silence. I didn't know how to talk about it or how to describe it so people could understand. So, I said nothing. I lost friends, businesses, our house, and our savings. After my deepest and longest depression, my wife and

I went from being successful members of the upper middle class, with a high-net worth, to being $250,000 in debt and battling repercussions that I still live with today. Now, triggers like an old song or a mention of one of our long vacations brings back memories of success and good health, but also guilt, anxiety, fear, and loathing.

After two months my wife Heather came to me and said, "Are you ready?" I said, "Yes". And then she said, "Pack some things and we'll leave." She was taking me to St. Vincent Hospital, but things were hazy, and I was confused. I thought we were going on vacation.

On the second day in the hospital, I met with a psychiatrist. He asked me how it was going. I said, "Not too bad, but the service here sucks. I ordered a margarita when I got here, and it still hasn't arrived." He looked at me and wrote something down on his notepad. Then he said, "Well, do you know where you are?" I said, "My wife said it was going to be a surprise. I'm hoping St. Thomas." "No" he said, "It's St. Vincent's." "Oh!" I said, "Better make that a rum mojito."

I had no idea where I was or what to expect at the hospital. I was really not well. But it was a safe place. No one could come see me because I didn't want to see anyone. I didn't have to worry about a knock at the door from a bill collector, or the ringing of the phone. I didn't have to worry about being judged. In the hospital I began to relax. The stress and anxiety began to lift.

I remember looking around the ward at other people and thinking, "I don't belong here. I am not like these other people." Four days later I looked around again and I realized, OMG that's me! I do belong here. And for some reason, at the exact same time, I thought of a joke.

So why do they keep the doors locked to the psychiatric unit?... Because there are so many people trying to get in.

Not long after that I thought of another joke. I wasn't making fun of anyone. My mind was dealing with the situation. I was in the right place. For those of us in the unit it was we, not them and me.

So... where do most injuries occur in the psychiatric unit? People fighting for position in the medication line... And that's just the nurses.

I was sent home from that first stay at the hospital too soon. They said my insurance company only wanted me there for seven days. I was nowhere near ready to leave. The day I got out, the darkness all came back. All the improvement from my hospital stay left me on the ride home. The beginnings of calmness, the beginnings of peace of mind, all of it disappeared. It was gone, and I was back in bed and on the couch where I started.

My anxiety and panic attacks would get triggered by just about anything. A phone call. A knock at the door. A car driving by. Even seeing the news on TV would remind me of the sanity that I had lost. The triggers would take me back to a bad time and I would relive the experience. I would feel the anxiety. I would feel the fear and dread. My heart would beat faster. My mind would race. I would start to sweat. It was like PTSD, and it was awful. This went on for years.

If anything was worse than depression, it was the mania.

Flights beyond the clouds: mania

The mania was this amazing flight among the clouds. Filled with ideas, I was brilliant, unstoppable. I thought fast, I talked fast, and I moved fast. It was in mania that I took foolish risks that almost ruined me and my wife, Heather. It was in mania where my greatest embarrassments and secrets were created. In mania, I decorated our Christmas tree with $10,000 worth of $100 bills. I felt great but it was crazy great.

It was in mania where I lost weight and had little interest in eating. Eating seemed like a waste of time. I had grandiose thoughts in both my business and personal life and chased them all day. At night there was little sleep. My mind raced and my heart pounded. I couldn't wait for the next day, so I could be brilliant again.

In mania, people were drawn to me. I was energetic and gregarious. I was the greatest salesman in the world. I borrowed money from banks and started businesses. I made lots of money for a while. I was a respected businessman. I was respected for my vision and success. In 1985 I co-founded a successful wholesale bakery. But then, it was in mania that I bought and owned six Subway Sandwich shops, started a bagel bakery and franchise company, and it was in mania where

I grew these businesses so fast that I ran out of money, then lost it all. There was no need to grow so fast, but that is what the mania told me to do. Mania pushed me over the top and broke my brain.

My mania switched from this calm euphoric feeling to feeling consumed with anxiety. My mind was out of control. I obsessed about everything, and sometimes I could not bring myself back to think of something I wanted to think about. My brain was on autopilot going 100 miles over the speed limit.

From depression to mania to incapacitation. I experienced it all and was unable to control any of it. What followed was 17 more years of pain and suffering. I was so lucky to have Heather. Without her I would have been on the street. Without my family I would be dead.

A true low point for me came years after being in the hospital. I was still depressed. Still disabled. I was just a shell of myself. I decided that since no meds had worked and no therapy had worked that I would try ECT, electro-convulsive therapy. Also known as shock therapy.

The treatment was at Oregon Health Sciences University. It is a great medical school, and they have great medical care. But it was an old building with narrow hallways and many floors. The ECT was in the basement down a dead-end hallway. It was cold and clinical.

The day of the treatment I went in and they had me change into a gown. The nurse took my vitals and then gave me a mild sedative to help me relax. When it was time for the treatment, they rolled me into a small room. I would soon be fully anesthetized. But first, to improve the connections to my brain, they gave me some nicotine in the I.V. I will never forget it. As it went into my vein, I could taste it. Somewhere between my nostrils and my tongue I could smell/taste it. That is the last thing I remember before I went under. I can still taste it like it was yesterday.

It was in desperation that I opted for shock therapy. I have a picture in my mind of being wired and shocked. In the old days there used to be body convulsions. That didn't happen to me, but my mind convulsed. My pathways were clear. My mind was reset.

The ECT worked. I felt better after the treatment. But one of the side effects is temporary memory loss. I would be driving to the pharmacy and end up at the post office. Or I would forget my way home. One time I even forgot I was married. Heather thought maybe that was not so bad after all.

Shock therapy worked so well that I got a portable shock therapy machine. It's called a taser. Now when I get depressed I just tase myself in the head. It works so well the people in my support group want me to tase them in the head too. I am thinking about charging a copay. (This is a joke. Don't try this at home.)

Transformation

Years later, I saw David Granirer perform. David is the creative and funny founder of Stand Up for Mental Health, a comic who speaks openly about his mental illness and tells jokes about his experiences. He also teaches stand-up comedy to folks with a mental illness.

When I saw him perform, I thought, "I could do that, I'm just as funny as he is. My jokes are as good as his." Maybe it was a manic moment when I saw him do his act, but his jokes reminded me of my jokes from the psychiatric unit at St. Vincent's Hospital in Portland.

I decided to take David's stand-up comedy class.

In David's class we took our bad experiences and challenges and looked for the humor in them. In comedy the more challenges you have, the more material you have for humor. Boy, did I have a lot of material.

The jokes I write are all based on the truth about living with mental illness. The basis of comedy is expectation and surprise. The set-up of a joke is based on the truth and creates an expectation of what comes next. The punch line is the creative part and the surprise. And the creative surprise is what makes us laugh. The more creative and the bigger the surprise, the more we laugh.

The transformative power of finding humor in the pain and writing jokes about the pain and suffering is amazing and cathartic. Week after week I would come up with serious stuff that I could make funny. Then I had to sound funny. When you are depressed, life feels flat, and so one thing I had to work on was not being monotone. I had had so many feelings of worthlessness during my depression that not only was my voice quiet, but it was flat. Flat is not good for comedy. Inflection keeps the audience interested and makes the jokes funnier.

The effect of comedy on me was like turning a depressed

caterpillar into a butterfly. I got off my belly and began to fly. No longer was I weighed down with guilt and suffering. I was free—free to be the real me that I hadn't been in years. It was amazing! I could talk to people about my mental illness. I would throw in a few jokes and it would disarm the fear. When they heard me talk about mental illness in a humorous way, their walls would come down and they would no longer look at me with pity or anxiety or fear.

I became a real person. My confidence rose. Just by being the new me, I could be a subtle stigma buster. People wanted to talk to me. They wanted to hear my jokes. They wanted to laugh with me. Our show at a NAMI National Convention in Seattle was in front of 300 people. It was recorded and went up on YouTube. I became somewhat of a celebrity in my small circle. Fifteen minutes of fame that helped reach a much larger audience with mental health comedy—busting stigma and communicating a message of transformation and hope that was now globally accessible.

Having bipolar disorder and anxiety is hard. But the anxiety is the worst part. The mania and the depression come and go. But the anxiety is constant. It is always there, and it is awful. One of the ways my anxiety manifested itself was that if I went into a public bathroom, and anyone else was in there, I couldn't go. I tried. But because of the anxiety I just couldn't go. Many times, I would stand at the urinal, and when I couldn't go, I faked it.

Then I would leave the bathroom and wait. Sometimes for five minutes. Sometimes for half an hour. I would wait until no one was left inside. And then I would go in and go.

Things slowly got better. And then last week Heather and I went to a movie. Afterwards I had to go so I went into the restroom. There were other people in there, but I went up to the urinal and went.

At that moment I realized how far I had come. I stepped back from the urinal, lifted my arms over my head, and yelled, "Yes! Yes! Yes!" The other people in the restroom looked at me like I was crazy. I said to myself, "No, not anymore."

After losing so many years to depression and mania, learning comedy helped me come back to myself. I started to look for the humor in my bad experiences. It is like I created new pathways in my brain to think about the terrible experiences. Instead of reliving the bad experiences, I reframed them.

One day I was driving by a restaurant and flashed back to losing everything. Then I saw the big sign. It said, "Happy Hour". I thought that's being discriminatory. There should also be a "Crappy Hour" for depressed people... And bipolar people could go to both.

In the hospital the doctor prescribed medication for my bipolar disorder. This med is notorious for the side effect of weight gain. True to form, while taking it I gained forty pounds. I decided to do something about it, so I joined a health club. I started doing the treadmill. But it didn't take long to realize that the treadmill is the perfect exercise for someone with a mental illness because you do the same thing over and over and over again, and you never get anywhere. Then one day I was working out and the guy next to me looked over and said, "You're not going very fast." I said, "That's okay. My mind's racing."

Having bipolar disorder makes having relationships hard. Like when you are dating someone, when do you tell them you have bipolar disorder? First date is too soon. Fourth date is too late. If you tell them on the second date, do they ghost you? And what do you say? "I really like you, and oh yeah by the way I'm crazy."

That's why I think there should be a dating service for folks with a mental illness. I can see the postings now. "Single white male seeks single white female to share compound in Idaho." Or how about, "Single female seeks male with no government connections." Or my favorite. "Dual personality female seeks dual personality male… for double dates."

Sure, all these years later, I still have times of depression and mania. It is better though. The lows are not so low, and they don't last as long. And the highs are not so high. Sometimes it is hard to recognize the ups and downs because they come on so slowly. But today I know the signs.

When someone is depressed, sex is the last thing they think of. When someone is manic, it seems as though sexual ideation is always part of it. So, I have figured out a sure way to know when I am depressed or manic. When I am

depressed, I spend all day trying to get out of bed. When I am manic, I spend all day trying to get Heather into bed.

Some things about mental illness are really hard to talk about. Suicide is one of them.

A few comics from some of my classes get together from time to time to share new material and just catch up. At one of these get togethers the topic of suicide came up. There were eight of us there. Every one of us experienced suicide ideation. We talked about our thoughts of suicide. None of us had attempted suicide, but we had all thought about it. We had all thought about how we would do it. We'd all weighed the pros and cons.

Some people say that you shouldn't talk about suicide because it will make someone more likely to do it. But the truth is the exact opposite. Talking about it brings it out in the open and makes it okay to think about. Knowing that others also think about it is actually a great relief. It helps you know that you are not alone. It helps to know that thinking about suicide does not make you a bad person. It helps to know that thinking about it does not mean you are going to do it.

The folks at our get-together talked about their ideations. We talked openly about different methods of suicide. We talked about the pluses and minuses. We talked about things that you could and would only say to fellow travelers. It was healthy. It was great, great therapy.

Suicide is never funny…except when it is. I tell a joke about it when I perform. At the beginning of the joke, I can feel the audience tense up a bit. They are thinking, "Is he really going to tell a joke about suicide?" "Can he do that?" I can and I do. Afterwards there is always the release of tension and laughter.

My wife is incredibly supportive of my mental health, and of my comedy. She shows it in different ways. Like one time when I was really low, things were bad, so I decided to end it all. I went into the bathroom and took a bunch of pills. Afterward I called my wife for help... She said there are more pills under the sink.

After my set, someone always comes up to me and tells me how much they loved the joke. They talk about their thoughts of suicide, sometimes for the first time. These are their thoughts that they can't talk about with anyone else. The joke gets these thoughts out into the open where they are less scary. Maybe the next time they have thoughts of suicide they will think of my joke, and it will bring a smile to their face, and lead to humor and healing instead of darkness and despair.

Humor and laughter have helped me live with my lost years and my hard times. I don't spend my day immersed in bad memories anymore. I find humor in something every day. I come up with jokes. Some good ones, some silly. Some are just right for my 10-year-old grandson. Like...

Why did the farmer cross the road?... To get his chicken.

And... what is the difference between a New York squirrel and an Oregon squirrel?... The accent.

After taking the comedy class and performing, I began to teach stand-up comedy to others with a mental illness. I'm good at it. What? Really? I know. This wasn't on my possible career list. It is not something I ever thought would be on my resume, and it sure wasn't on my bucket list. Sometimes life just happens.

I have taught a lot of comedy classes to people at varying levels of their mental illness. One group I taught was a group at the Oregon State Mental Hospital. I taught the class to forensic patients, meaning those who have committed a crime and been sentenced to the hospital instead of jail, guilty except for insanity.

A joke among the patients is that it is hard to get in. But it is much harder to get out. Often the patients spend more time locked in the hospital than they would have in prison. The Psychiatric Security Review Board is tough.

After teaching the class I was able to add to my resume that I taught stand-up comedy to the criminally insane. But the truth is that most people in the state hospital are as sane as anyone. They were funny too.

One patient jokes:

"When I die, I can't decide whether to get buried or get cremated, so my headstone is going to read, 'Rest in Pieces'."

Another patient who was obsessed with suicide said that since being in the hospital his thoughts of suicide are getting better.

"Now when I visualize myself jumping off the Golden Gate Bridge, I'm wearing a floaty."

Finding humor in everyday experiences is important for me. And living in Oregon and being aware of the environment is a way of life. One day when I was depressed, I realized that being depressed is good for the environment. Who knew?

I read a story that said Americans are showering way too often. Apparently, we should only shower once a week. Any more than that and we are wasting water. Not to mention washing essential oils off or our bodies and out of our hair. That made me laugh, and think "Wow, with my bipolar depression I am way ahead of this curve." It gave me a whole new way of looking at myself.

When I get depressed, taking a shower is one of the first things that goes. Once a week? Heck, how about once a month. Think of how much water and soap I am saving. This is good for the environment, right?

I also save on other grooming products. I have no need for hair gel, and little for deodorant. I didn't realize how eco-friendly I am thanks to my depressive episodes. And not just because I'm not taking a shower.

When I am depressed, I wear the same clothes day after day. Sometimes I sleep in my clothes because it is easier than taking them off and putting them back on again. Smart, right?

Add to that that I can't get off the couch to put clothes in the washer and doing laundry every other month or so becomes a reality. Running the washing machine less saves water and keeps laundry detergent out of the sewers.

But wait, there's more. When I am depressed, it is all I can do to get something to eat. I don't have an appetite, and when I do eat it has to be fast and easy. Cereal is my go-to item. It's perfect. No cooking, and it's easy to reuse the bowl and spoon after a quick rinse. Talk about reducing my carbon footprint.

When I am in the midst of my bipolar depression during the colder months, I spend many of my days on the couch wrapped up in a blanket. I don't have to turn up the heat, so I save on energy consumption. I'm not getting out of the house to shop either, so I am in tune with the mantra reduce, reuse, and recycle.

In the depths of my depression I can't work, so I can't afford a car, and I end up walking or taking the bus. Less driving means fewer emissions. It also means less gas usage, less need for motor oil, and less usage of windshield washer fluid and antifreeze. Tires last longer too. I am going to count that as another plus in the being good to the environment column.

Perhaps this idea struck me because I live near Portland, which is a very environmentally conscious city. If there were a contest for the greenest person in town, I think I would win. Who else is going to admit that they only shower once a month, do laundry every other month, sleep in their clothes, and eat from the same dish every day?

We always need to promote a more positive view of people with mental illness. So, in the future, when someone asks me what I do, I will tell them I am saving the planet. When someone asks why I have disappeared from sight for three months, I will tell them I am reducing my carbon footprint. And when someone says that I am not being very sociable, I will just tell them, "Yeah, but I am environmentally friendly."

Living with bipolar disorder has been extremely hard. I have had dark days and lost years. I have lost friends, been homeless, and almost lost my family. Finding humor in my hardship has helped me cope. It changed my outlook and helps me deal with the flashbacks. I still live with depression, and I still live with mania, but when they come, they don't incapacitate me.

People living with mental illness are coming out of the mental health closet. It is okay to talk about it. It is okay to write about it. And fortunately for me, it is okay to laugh about it.

When I was first diagnosed my kids were young and Heather and the kids and I sat at the kitchen table and talked about it. The next day my daughter Meghan went to school. In art she was drawing, and the teacher came up and said, "Meghan, what are you drawing?" Meghan said, "It's a bipolar bear." "Oh," said the teacher, "Can you tell me about it?" And Meghan said, "It is white, it lives at the North Pole, and it takes Prozac."

CHAPTER 2

LORAYNE

I have PTSD, bipolar depression, and anxiety.
That means that on a good day I'm creatively depressed
with a sense of dread while having a panic attack.
—Lorayne

If you sat next to Lorayne on a bus, you'd see a little old lady sporting practical clothes and sensible, short gray hair, wearing an oxygen tank and carrying a cane. If for any reason you found yourself exchanging standard bus pleasantries along the lines of "Excuse me, is anyone sitting here?" you'd hear the cheerful but straightforward, no-nonsense tones of someone who prescribes to the life philosophy of earlier generations. Sort of an "It is what it is and I'm making the best of it" kind of an approach. You'd make sure you weren't crowding her, since she seems a little fragile, and you'd go back to reading your book or checking Facebook on your smartphone.

You would be missing out on one tough, fascinating cookie. You would never know you were in the presence of a formidable fighter who has triumphed over severe mental illness for more than 40 years, most of those years spent steadily working taxing physical jobs. Lorayne was an extreme preemie born long before those babies were supposed to survive, and she's been gluten-free since before gluten was discovered and LONG before it was trendy. She is a two-time cancer survivor, a passionate community volunteer for the less fortunate, a sexual assault survivor, a life-long student who is still learning new skills, and one heck of a comedian.

Some SMH comedians are quite upfront that they perform for the laughs, for the attention, or for the chance to be up on stage. *(Well, at least Tara does.)* But not Lorayne. For Lorayne, it's all about being understood. She is doing it so her family will see her — really see — and understand her. "I want my family to know who I am, and what makes me tick." She also does it so that you will see and better understand her and all people with mental illness.

Lorayne isn't one to use more words than necessary. At this point in her life, she doesn't have the patience or the oxygen. But Lorayne speaks to something which is inherently human: the desire to be known, to be recognized and granted worth by others. Don't we all want that?

Yet too often people living with mental illness experience exactly the opposite – they are unknown, they are ignored, and they are marginalized and misunderstood.

"Comedy and being part of this book are another way for me to do advocacy," Lorayne says, "for people like me to show people we can do more than people think. It allows me to express to the community that people with mental illness can and do, do stuff every day."

I was born in 1951 as a one-and-a-half-pound preemie. I spent the first year of my life in an incubator up at Doernbecher Hospital, and I died several times. But I kept coming back. And for this life??? Seriously...

I'm convinced that from the beginning, I've always been discharged from the hospital too early. I've been trying to get back in ever since.

A rough childhood

Lorayne was a preemie in 1951, born with underdeveloped lungs, hearing problems and many other related health issues at a time before preemies were expected to even survive. She was born fourth of eight kids—two girls and six boys—and she was the first girl.

In some families, the sickly Lorayne might have become the sick little princess, at the center of attention. In her home? Not so much. Not only was Lorayne often sick, but she was a tomboy, and definitely not her mother's dream of a "girly" girl. As a child Lorayne was shy and lonely, even in a home full of kids. She was always different. She never fit in.

Her mom put her in beauty schools and dancing classes, all attempts to change her into who her mother wanted Lorayne to be, but to no avail. Discipline at home was harsh, old-school, and sometimes physically abusive. Thoughts of escape came often, but she had nowhere to go.

She had celiac disease and the resulting extreme dietary needs *(back in the day when no one had heard of "gluten-free")* further exiled Lorayne from family life and family events. Her brother Steve has clear memories of Lorayne at special family meals, even Thanksgiving and Christmas dinners, sitting down to a plate of egg whites, skim milk and cottage cheese.

Lorayne's mental illness was far less obvious, even though it began to affect her in her teens. When asked when he knew about Lorayne's mental health issues, or when the family began talking about it, Steve said it wasn't talked about when they were kids. Steve is the oldest of Lorayne's siblings, and he left home at 18 for the military followed by a family and a career. He says he was not even aware that Lorayne had mental illness until they were both well into adulthood.

It seems clear now that Lorayne's mother, who was hospitalized at times, also lived with mental illness, although it was rarely discussed and she was never diagnosed. Steve and Lorayne both reiterate that at that time, families just didn't talk about it. Lorayne believes that today her mother would also be diagnosed with bipolar disorder. Her mother's illness, combined with what her mother perceived as Lorayne's failure to be the little girl she'd hoped for, led to a very tense and difficult relationship.

More pain came in her early twenties when she was sexually assaulted by a family friend. He came over one Saturday and sent the other kids to relatives. He told her he was going to teach her how the world works. That's when he raped her. A brother who knew about the attack blamed Lorayne, making horrible accusations that she would hear echoing in her head for decades to follow.

The pain and the guilt were too much and Lorayne began to experience severe symptoms of post-traumatic stress disorder (PTSD). She suffered in silence. She didn't tell the rest of her family because she believed they would not support her. That's when the panic attacks started, horrible anxiety that has been her cruel partner ever since.

As bad as things were at home, they weren't much better at school. It didn't help that she was always a poor student who struggled academically, and because she was a generally quiet kid, she just ... slipped through the cracks.

I always felt different growing up, even though I didn't get diagnosed with mental illness until I was in my twenties. In high school while other girls were wondering if their bra strap was showing, I was wondering if my bipolar was showing. Could people tell just by looking at me? How about now? (Turns from side to side.) How about now?

Seriously, I look back and there were signs. One time when I was in high school, we went on a retreat to the monastery at Mt. Angel. I was bored, up alone at 5 a.m., my mind was racing, and I wanted to have some fun.

So, I climbed up the bell tower and grabbed the bell. I wrapped my hands around one side and my legs around the other and started swinging back and forth. It gave new meaning to the word bong.

Mental illness

Lorayne left home right after high school, starting a long career of strenuous physical jobs, including about 10 years working in nursing homes and then two different factory jobs for twenty years. One pivotal trauma came early in Lorayne's career. She was working in a nursing home, and the care in the facility was terrible. Unfortunately, her own grandfather lived there at the time. She would go to her grandfather's room after her shifts each day to try to coax him to eat, as none of the other staff would take the time, and she was afraid he was starving. Sadly, one day as she was feeding him, he choked to death, dying right in front of Lorayne.

That trauma triggered Lorayne's first serious episode of mental illness, and her first commitment to Dammasch State Hospital, the notorious Oregon state mental facility made famous in "One Flew Over the Cuckoo's Nest." She was 24 years old, and it was 1975. She experienced a manic episode at work, or had a "breakdown," losing awareness only to wake up, committed, in the lock-down psychiatric hospital ward.

When I was finally diagnosed in 1975, I was actually working as a nurse's aide in a hospital. But I started freaking out, so they wanted to sedate me.

I said "oh, no you're not, you're not gonna poke me, you can just shoot up this orange I brought for lunch." I guess they missed the orange 'cause I woke up the next day at Dammasch, the state mental hospital.

I've been in the state mental hospital six times. But I must have been pretty good at it. They kept inviting me back.

Lorayne was diagnosed at Dammasch with bipolar disorder, though back then they called it manic depression. According to the National Institute of Mental Health, "Bipolar disorder, also known as manic-depressive illness, is a brain disorder that causes unusual shifts in mood, energy, and activity levels, and the inability to carry out day-to-day tasks." Lorayne looks back now and sees signs of her mania as early as adolescence, when she would go without sleep for days at a time, "always just making candles or other weird stuff."

This first commitment lasted about three months. Still to this day she isn't sure exactly. She lost track of time.

Lorayne's kind, considerate nature got her a job while inside the hospital. She walked or escorted people in wheelchairs across the campus to a particular door. A nurse would take them in while Lorayne waited outside. She didn't know this was where shock therapy took place. She just knew that when people came out, they didn't talk, and she escorted them back to their room in silence.

Lorayne was always helpful, once even giving in to the pleas of a roommate by helpfully pushing her out a tiny window in the hospital to her freedom.

The kindness was often one-sided, and rarely returned. She saw a lot of nasty stuff done to patients in Dammasch, as mental health treatment in 1975 was still harsh and primitive. It was hard to take, and she was unable to do anything about it for fear of retaliation. She vowed she would never go back.

Unfortunately, that was not the way it would work out. She was committed five more times before Dammasch was closed for good in 1995.

After her first stay, Lorayne refused the doctor's advice to go home to her family where she knew she would not do well. So, she was sent to live in a women's dormitory in downtown Portland near what is now Portland State University. She learned a lot there about the world, living and navigating the "big city" fresh from lock-up. She liked all of the activity, but she was still not well. For fun she would throw fruit out the window aiming for the people walking on the sidewalk below. She had a roommate but did not like her. One time, Lorayne tied the roommate's shoelaces together. Even now, that's about as vindictive as Lorayne gets. She's too nice, too considerate, to do anything more.

I earned a lot of privileges when I was at the state hospital. I even had a job walking the other patients from their rooms to different appointments. I didn't realize at the time where I was taking them, just that they always came back drooling. I finally figured out they weren't hungry; I'd been walking them to electroshock therapy.

I still see one of them, a lady, around town, but I'm guessing a fond reunion isn't in the cards.

Not that she recognizes me.

Or her husband.

Or the need for pants ...

Once when I was in the state psychiatric hospital my roommate wanted me to help her escape. So I obliged.

She asked me to push her out the window. Well, she was a big gal, and this was a small window. But finally, I pushed her through. Too bad we were on the eighth floor.

It worked out OK though. She landed on her head.

After she bounced right up, she took off running for the fence. If she could get over it, she was free. Then there was trouble. Right when she got to the top, her clothes got caught on the wire. But it didn't deter her. She fell over the other side. Buck naked. Then she began singing her rendition of "Born Free."

Lorayne is quick to proudly point out her long, productive work history, and she is fully aware it is an accomplishment that puts her among a minority of people with severe mental illness. Lorayne is also unusual in that she never self-medicated with alcohol or drugs. Despite her mental illness and her history of trauma, Lorayne managed 30 years of productivity and many jobs over her working life, particularly impressive for a person in Lorayne's generation with severe mental illness. She and her contemporaries came of age at a time when chronic, severe mental illness too often lead to a life of institutionalization or homelessness, before recovery was a real hope.

She says she is forever grateful for the person who first told her about the job safety guaranteed to her through the Family Medical Leave Act (FMLA) of 1993. She says her jobs were saved by that law many times, allowing her to keep her job while receiving treatment for her mental illness.

Lorayne has never married or had children. No children because she didn't want them to end up like her; she didn't want any kids to know the misery and sickness that she had known. No marriage because she didn't want a man to walk out on her. There were no high school sweethearts. No formal dates. No boyfriends. No great loves.

These kids today, they think mental illness is so hard, I've seen things that would make them cry into their Prozac.

Really, I'm telling ya, these kids today, they think it's so hard, I've seen things that would make them beg for a gentle Taser tap from the Portland Police Department.

Now, my bipolar is like an elevator. Up and down, up and down. Going up I feel good, going down I feel lousy. One time I got stuck on the 13th floor.

Nobody found me for weeks.

Life is still tough

Lorayne's mental illness never went away; in fact, it got worse. The voices in her head grew louder, her mind racing uncontrollably. She was not sleeping. In 2001 when she was working at an industrial parts manufacturer, her illness required yet another hospitalization. That's where she was when her employer called and told her not to come back. Devastated, she fell deeper into depression.

Severe physical and mental health problems had taken their toll, and finally in 2002, Lorayne was forced to retire and go on disability. Even that, however, was not easy. She was denied disability three times before being granted the benefit.

This is not an uncommon delay for people with mental illness.

Lorayne's physical problems could be categorized as impressively depressing, if it were not for the matter-of-fact way she ticks them off. She has serious gastrointestinal issues, including celiac disease; foot problems which make walking painful and difficult; asthma exacerbated by a working lifetime of various chemical exposures in factory jobs; hearing problems; and generally poor health from her start in life as a preemie. Lorayne has also had skin cancer and two bouts of breast cancer, and she was gluten-free long before it was hip at Whole Foods.

Symptoms of mental illness are still very much a part of daily life for Lorayne. She has flashbacks from past trauma that cause her to curl up in small spaces like her bathroom with a pillow and blanket for long periods of time. She experiences racing, tormenting thoughts, including a repeating loop of hurtful past statements from attackers or family members over and over again, horrible things like "women deserve to be raped." She is currently seeing a therapist and participates in a dialectical behavioral therapy (DBT) support group.

One time I attempted suicide with aspirin. It wasn't very effective, but my headache was gone.

Another day I felt like I had a terrible taste in my mouth so I drank some bleach to get rid of it. Then I had to go to the emergency room. The nurse asked me why I drank bleach. I said it does a better job than Scrubbing Bubbles.

I'm much better writing jokes when I am manic.
Of course, they don't make sense until I am depressed.

Healing and advocacy through comedy

Today, Lorayne lives with PTSD, anxiety, and bipolar disease. She has been actively involved as a volunteer with NAMI for about 20 years, and it was through NAMI that she heard about SMH. Even with mental illness and her physical challenges, she wanted to try stand-up comedy. She wanted to do something to change the dark hole she was in.

Lorayne figured it would be another way for her to show the world that "people living with mental illness can do stuff and we don't have to be locked up; we can get better and get on with our life."

Lorayne is hardly the type of person most would envision doing stand-up comedy. In fact, she hadn't been a big fan of comedy prior to SMH. Before her first performance, she had never even seen a Stand Up for Mental Health show. She'd certainly never seen herself as particularly funny, or as someone who would be good at comedy. Previously, she'd just been offended when she'd heard jokes about people being crazy or having mental illness.

"When I first came to the classes, I was leery about whether I'd be able to come up with jokes," she says. But they say the more struggles you have, the more material you have for jokes. Lorayne may have been overqualified. Especially with her bipolar disorder. Writing jokes with Dave, Tara and the group came easily, and "the way it was taught, my jokes just flowed like water."

As Lorayne waited for her turn to go onstage at her first show, she was scared. Scared she wouldn't be able to do it. Afraid she would tell her jokes and no one would laugh. She was scared she would fall on her face and she was also afraid she would literally fall off the stage.

Then it was time. "And now, welcome to the stage… Lorayne!" The audience grew quiet, as Lorayne stood up and used her cane to get to the stage, slowly, painfully making it up the steps to the microphone. They were anxious, as if they could not imagine this frail lady successfully telling jokes and making them laugh.

There was a hush as Lorayne began. She was nervous. The crowd was nervous.

She spoke. Quietly at first. But she found she was fine standing alone on stage. Maybe it shouldn't have been surprising, she'd been alone most all her life. As she spoke her voice got louder and the audience stopped being nervous about the frail lady with bipolar disorder and they started to laugh. About two minutes in she hit her stride. Her voice grew strong as the crowd's laughter confirmed that her jokes were funny.

The more jokes she told, the more comfortable the audience became and the more they laughed. You could see the twinkle come into her eyes. The audience was with her and she knew it. She nailed the end of the act, the last "ROAR" in the last punchline booming out of her tiny body with power.

All the comics from the show that night got applause. But the applause for Lorayne was louder and longer. The audience sensed that they had just seen something special, more than a frail little lady telling jokes. They saw a victory and a milestone. A transformation.

Afterward? She was pleasantly surprised and proud that she'd pulled it off.

For Lorayne, the hardest part of the show is volume, being sure she is loud enough to be heard and understood, as well as hitting the punch lines and the funny parts at the right time and hitting the critical "ROAR" at the end of her act just right.

Her favorite part of the show is getting people to laugh about something they might think is so depressing or sad, and breaking the crusty shell many people have about mental illness.

She also has enjoyed watching the growth of the other comics, including Shaun, a cognitively impaired comic whom she has known since he was a boy, coaching him in Special Olympics. "It was nice to see him step up and try it, neat also that someone like Martin who has autism stepped up to do it," she says. "It breaks a lot of stigmas."

Comedy has given Lorayne a confidence and an openness that she had never had before. She now talks to other people she wouldn't have talked to before, about her life and about what she's been through. "I can come out about my stuff now; I don't have to hide behind a door."

I take a lot of meds. I have my morning meds and my nighttime meds. I even have a memory med to help me remember to take my meds.

Proud big brother sees her now

The confidence and openness Lorayne has earned through

her comedy journey have paid off in the growth of new and deeper relationships. Lorayne's brother, Steve, was at her first performance at Marylhurst, and Lorayne doesn't believe she and her brother would have found their way back to each other or to the close relationship they now share without her comedy and SMH. A sister was also able to see it on video later. Lorayne says it felt different to finally have family members really see her, really listen, and hear about her experiences.

After the show there was a line of folks waiting to meet her and congratulate her. One of the people in line was Steve.

Lorayne and her brother had never been close, though there wasn't the bad blood with him that there had been with other siblings. That night her brother was beaming. You could see it on his face, "You go, girl." They hugged for the first time in years. Lorayne's eyes watered, and she held on tight, soaking up every bit of love there was in that hug.

"This was my first attempt to tell any of my family what I've been through. It made it possible for me to talk to Steve about it. He came to the show, and afterward he came up and put his arm around my shoulder and said I did a good job. He was amazed at what I've been through, didn't know about the abuse, the reactions or the comments I'd gotten from other family members."

Steve confirms that this is true. Most of the stories Lorayne shares in her act are new to Steve. Through most of their lives, Steve and Lorayne were somewhat distant, typical for siblings separated by age and seasons of life. Steve didn't really get to know Lorayne until they were both well into adulthood, and not until his recent retirement.

While Steve's relative lack of awareness of Lorayne's life —not even knowing about most of her hospitalizations — may seem strange, it is really not surprising and illustrates a couple of important truths. First, it was common for earlier generations to not talk about mental illness. It would not have been at all unusual for a busy older brother with his own life and family to have been largely unaware of what his much younger sister was going through.

Second, frequent bouts of depression and hospitalizations also increase isolation, as does the tendency to conceal mental illness. Once isolated, it can be nearly impossible for a person living with mental illness to build those bridges back to family relationships.

But those bridges often lead to priceless experiences and increased quality of life. The performance night initiated Steve and Lorayne's new relationship, a relationship that basically did not exist before her comedy journey. Indeed, Lorayne and Steve are both clear that their newfound closeness has enriched both of their lives.

Lorayne now knows love from a family member, something she thought she would never have. She is not so lonely anymore and day-to-day difficulties are a little bit easier. All because she was brave enough to say "yes, I will give stand-up comedy a try." There have been other transformations within our comedy troupe, but few as special or as dramatic as Lorayne's.

Meanwhile, it has allowed Steve to reclaim a sister who once felt lost to him, a sister whose courage in facing the challenges in her life is an inspiration. Watching the show, he says,

"I was real proud of her. Lorayne has had such an ordeal just to live, it's amazing she's still got a sense of humor." He was surprised by how well she performed, and freely admits he doesn't know if he could get up in front of all of those people. When asked what he thought of the other comedians, he says that honestly, he didn't get much out of any of the other performances because he was so focused on Lorayne and nervous for her performance.

Since the Marylhurst show, Steve has remained focused on reconnecting with his younger sister. Lorayne now sees her big brother at least three to four times a week. Steve enjoys spending time with her and helping when he can to make her life a little easier – driving her to medical appointments, taking her for frozen yogurt, sometimes just sitting together by the river, watching it flow by.

In addition to the big transformations, there are also little victories. From Steve's perspective, there was always lots of teasing and joking around in their large family of eight kids, but that wasn't always a big part of who Lorayne was. Until recently, Steve says, he didn't feel that Lorayne saw much humor in her situation, and she was definitely a different person, not as prone to laugh, really shy and quiet. Now he says, "I can joke around with her and she's OK with it."

Steve hopes that the humor in Lorayne's stand-up act and in Stand Up for Mental Health will humanize those with mental illness. He hopes it helps people see Lorayne and others with mental illness as just people who have illnesses like any other illness. He feels strongly that mental illness is simply a physical illness of the organ that is the brain, and that it should not result in people being treated any differently than those with other physical ailments.

"I think she's a remarkable woman. It's great that even with everything else she's got going on, she's able to help others. I'm very proud of my sister and very glad this has helped brighten up her life. She deserves it."

Her new relationship with her siblings has benefited Lorayne in other areas of her life as well. Now Steve has power of attorney over her affairs, and her sister is the representative for her mental health directive. Recently she completed her advanced directives, a step which, given the severity of her physical illnesses, has left her a feeling of peace and accomplishment about her last days, whenever they may be.

Peace, accomplishment, and Lorayne-style practicality. "No machines," she says about the end of her life. "When the time comes, just keep me comfortable. I started my life on machines for a whole year, I don't want it to end the same way."

Lorayne has led a long life full of struggle in her sixty-plus years, and retirement might bring a fatalistic acceptance for some people along the lines of "this is how it is; I give up, I can't change now."

Not Lorayne. She continues to work for recovery and for peace, to learn more in order to get better. In addition to being engaged in both individual and group therapy, she participates regularly in an art therapy group. She has even explored creative writing. One key issue for Lorayne is that she is now in safe, stable housing. This allows her to control her environment and therefore her stress, making life easier.

As if that wasn't enough, Lorayne also continues to work hard for others. She volunteers to help train local Crisis Intervention Teams, teaching and advising parole and police officers how to interact with people with mental illness. She takes shifts at a local food pantry, she continues to coach the Special Olympic bowling team she's worked with for years, and she helps out at NAMI whenever she can. "My volunteer work also helps my recovery, helps me feel better."

After her first show, she became something of a local NAMI celebrity. People often ask her when she is doing another show. She always says "Soon," and she continues to perform her stand-up routine whenever she gets a chance. She has now done several comedy shows, and her fantasy is to do one for workers in the mental health field to change the way they see their clients.

Lorayne is no longer a shy wallflower. She strives every day to make things better for the people around her, and she truly cares about others with a mental illness. Stand-up comedy gave her a way to do that. At 61 Lorayne became a comic, and now she continues to be open to new experiences and new ways to make a difference.

And on the bad days? "Sure," she says. "There are days when I get bogged down by all of my problems, my physical illnesses and my mental health. Now I just go back to my comedy routine to remind myself, give myself a different perspective to help get me out of the hole I'm in."

I used to just be a survivor and not a fighter. I lived my life quietly for years, letting other people make decisions for

me, and then a great doctor finally helped me find my voice. Unfortunately, my voice sounded like Darth Vader.

My family didn't know how to take that, so they left me at the hospital and went home to get a gag order.

Now I'm a survivor and a fighter. My name is Lorayne, hear me roar (loud roar!). I've been in the state mental hospital six times, had cancer twice, been made fun of, been a victim of stigma, discrimination, and bullying. But I'm a survivor. I am a board member for my local chapter of the National Alliance on Mental Illness (NAMI). I did Crisis Intervention Training for the Clackamas County Sheriff's Office. I do NAMI "In Our Own Voice" presentations, and I'm on the affordable housing board. I help at the food bank once a month and I deliver food boxes to seniors and the disabled... And they say I'm crazy?! ROAR!!!

CHAPTER 3

MARTIN

Some words of advice:
If you are going to borrow money, borrow it from a
pessimist. He never expects to get it back.
—Martin

It's easier to learn about Martin from other people, specifically the people in his life who love him. While most of us can
go on and on for hours if asked to talk about ourselves *(at least*
Tara can) that's not easy for Martin. As he explains it, it's part
of his disability, or special ability. "You know, some people believe that people with autism don't have feelings, but I do. Not
many people with my disability have normal feelings, but I'm
not without feelings. What's unique about me is that I don't
always know what I'm feeling."

So, like many people on the autism spectrum, Martin isn't

that good at talking about himself or about what motivates him, or how an experience has changed him. But if we started with what his loved ones think about Martin, we would risk missing Martin on Martin, and missing how the larger world encounters him. So, we'll start with Martin. He'd heard about the SMH class from his dad, who had encouraged him to join, and he thought "Why not, I do like to be funny, and if I'm so into comedy why not do this?"

He would probably appreciate being described as tall, dark, and handsome, and it's also true. The dark-haired young man in his early 20's, who resembles actor Johnny Galecki *(Leonard on "The Big Bang Theory")*, came into the first SMH class and promptly separated himself from the group, planting himself in the corner of a couch on the outskirts of the room, away from the table around which the others gathered.

For the first three or four weeks, Martin sat on that couch across the room as the rest of the group sat at the table and shared bits of their stories and worked on their comedy. It took him a while to get used to the environment and the process of creating comedy. Once in a while he would pop off something totally unrelated to the topic of discussion. Dave would say, "That's interesting, Martin. Thanks for sharing." And he would grow quiet again, his focus returning back inside his own mind.

In conversation, Martin looks around furtively, often not making eye contact except for a half-second at a time. When answering questions, he pauses frequently, allowing his mind time to work, and his answers are brief and often require follow-up. But if you keep talking, Martin's pauses become shorter and he becomes more engaged. By the fifth week of class, Martin was ready, comfortable, and willing to participate. Sometimes in class it took Martin a long time to say something, but the group was patient and quiet while he was thinking and didn't interrupt. It was like there was a code in the group, all people with their own varying issues and disabilities, to be respectful of what others said and did and how they said and did it.

When I first started the comedy group I sat, looking down, and wouldn't say anything.
Now they can't get me to shut up ...
But the duct tape helps.

Martin's early reserve wasn't related to his fellow comedy students or their severe mental illness. When asked if he'd been concerned about that, he says, "Working with people with disabilities is nothing new to me. Of course, unlike people with some disabilities, I come off as a normal guy."

(Truth be told, Martin doesn't exactly come off as a normal guy, but in our group that's generally considered a plus. He does consider himself a funny guy though, and there we are in agreement.)

Martin's thoughts on being funny — or not — are perceptive. "The thing about my autism is, I pay attention to details other people don't notice, and I speak my mind, and sometimes it comes off as funny. But what I notice about myself is that sometimes I'm funny without meaning to be, or I could tell a joke and no one would get it. That's OK," because, he says, "It's better to feel like a funny guy than it is to be funny on command."

Sometimes the least funny guy in the room is the one trying the hardest to "Be Funny Right Now." Martin's more laid-back about humor. "When writing comedy it's better to have it hit you, so you just feel it," he says. "It's easier than if you have to go look for it."

Relaxed and chill is actually Martin's modus operandi, if you will. "I like to consider myself nice and laid-back, I don't worry about much. I'm just taking life by the horns, that's my motto, taking life by the horns." Yeah, the horns thing is his motto, laid back is his modus operandi.

Each week in class, Martin got more comfortable, and he started sharing material to turn into jokes. He says, "The class was a very unique experience; I got more than I expected out of it. I expected we'd just be jokin' around and thinking of stuff to make jokes. It turned out to be more than that, and I was really impressed with some of the other people's material." The change as he opened up was nothing less than amazing. Not only did he help with his own jokes, he helped others with theirs and fully participated in the process. For Martin, learning how to do stand-up comedy involved learning more about what was funny, what would make people laugh, and learning how to build a joke.

"As a comedian," Martin explains, "you've got to know when that moment is, when and when not to make a joke or make fun of something. So, I wouldn't make a joke about big things, like falling to your death, but about little misfortunes, or things that seem big and turn out not to be such a big deal."

A guy after Jerry Seinfeld's own heart.

One thing about being autistic is that my memory is really good.
It's so good SIRI asks ME questions.
My doctor said my mind is photographic but not photogenic. So, I make up for it with Photoshop.

Martin continued to blossom as his first show got closer, and he amazed the class by memorizing his act. He rehearsed well and it was obvious he was spending time with it away from the group.

The night of the performance the comedians were all nervous, for themselves and for each other. Yet Martin seemed calm. He confirms this. "I wasn't really nervous," he says, "I'm not really the nervous type. I knew I could knock'em dead, it was a matter of confidence."

During dress rehearsal he was good except for some minor things, like remembering how long to pause between jokes, to wait for laughs, regular stuff all of the comedians needed to remember. He hung out, yucking it up with the other comics as they all waited nervously for show time. Finally, the lights dimmed, and the show began.

Martin was up fifth. He strode to the microphone, looked down and paused, and then looked out at the audience. With a sly smile he told his first joke. "If you are going to borrow money, borrow it from a pessimist. He never expects to get it back." The audience laughed, and Martin was off and running.

The audience sat patiently, as without notes Martin

paused for several seconds at a time, searching for the jokes in his mind. It was amazing. They seemed instinctively to know that they were seeing Martin working hard and that even with the pause, Martin would be back with them in a moment, telling his next joke with perfect timing. The silence was not uncomfortable. It was just the way it was, and everyone knew it and accepted it. His face went from sly to serious and back to a bit devious as he went through his act, and he seemed to look at no one and everyone at the same time.

I'm writing a book. It's called "Autism for Dummies."
It's targeting a very small audience;
I don't know any dumb people with autism.

About halfway through he told this great joke about writing "Autism for Dummies." The audience really laughed, and we could just see the twinkle in his eye and the smile on his face. He was having fun. In fact, he recalls, "During the performance I felt like 'I'm enjoying this; I could keep'em entertained for hours. I could stay up here 'til midnight!' "

At the beginning of the SMH program, the class had met a quiet, disconnected young man who barely spoke, and then only in cryptic comments that rarely connected with the moment. But this guy onstage? This was a comedian who was fully in the moment. In the middle of his act he recognized someone in the audience, commented on it, and went on with his set. The next joke was about his dad, so he pointed out his dad in the crowd like an old pro, like a comic who'd been working the crowds for years!

We have fun in comedy class.

One week we decided to play cards. It didn't work though. Nobody was playing with a full deck.

Upon Martin's final joke, there was more laughter and then applause. With a wide smile, Martin confidently strode off the stage. He'd nailed it. He'd not only nailed it, but he'd loved it. "Doing the performance, it was definitely fun for me. I don't know about everyone else." He enjoyed the positive feedback, too. "Afterward people came up and said 'You were awesome. You were good. Why not take it to Comedy Central?' But I don't know about going that far. As far as the moment was concerned, I thought, 'oh you are just being kind.'"

Wilda, a friend of the family, was there that night, clapping and crying with pride, definitely NOT just being kind. She'd never imagined that she would see Martin be able to do something like this. She had known Martin's dad for 15 years, and Martin for about 10. She is a retired business professional and community advocate, and there are a couple of members of her wider family with mental health issues.

Wilda is a big Martin fan, and she'd been a little nervous about a comedy show about mental illness. Would it be respectful? Would it be funny? *(These are common pre-show concerns from our audiences, and thankfully they leave with a solid "Yes" to both questions.)* "When I first heard of it," she says, "I thought, 'Wow, how can that be? All these folks with mental illness poking fun at their illnesses and making others laugh?' When I saw the show, I was immensely impressed with the skill of the presenters, and with the stories they shared. I understood more about a variety of mental illnesses and what folks go through who have them. And, as I thought he would be, Martin was wonderfully funny, in a thought-provoking way."

When I was young, I played baseball. One time I hit the ball so far that 24 hours later it came around and hit me in the back of the head ... It hurt pretty bad.

So my parents took me to the emergency room.

When the doctor asked me what happened, I said that I hit a baseball so far that 24 hours later it came around and hit me in the back of the head.

He said, "My God, that's the third one this week."

Martin's parents, Joe and Colleen, were also at the show. Martin's dad, Joe, works in community relations and government relations for a local school district, and is as effusive with his words as his son is reserved. Martin also has a younger brother, Patrick, who is in college.

Joe was nervous before Martin's first performance. "It was all about Martin for me, that first performance. I'm sure the other people were great, but I was just thinking about Martin. Was he ok, was he nervous?" Watching his son perform stand up for the first time was emotional, nerve-wracking, and joyful as he watched Martin achieve a goal he'd set for himself years earlier.

Martin's mom, Colleen, as mothers do, worried about what could go wrong. "I thought he might get upset if things didn't go well, and he might not be able to bounce back. But he did fine."

His parents marvel at the changes they've seen in Martin since he has studied and performed stand-up comedy with SMH, things like Martin's growing ability to pick his first joke of a set based on the moment and what he is perceiving. He's now able to engage with the audience a bit, check out the room. Most importantly, he's no longer stuck inside himself as much, but now he's looking around at his world and making fun of things.

Logos yes, conversation no

His folks had known early on Martin was different. Martin had certain advanced abilities as a toddler, including the ability to memorize and mimic what he had heard and then, by preschool, what he had read. He could decode difficult words with ease and would memorize vast quantities of information and whole books at a time. But he couldn't have conversations or relate to the people around him. After a day spent running errands with his mom, Martin couldn't tell you what they'd done or where they'd been, but he could relay every logo he'd seen on the way on a sign or advertisement or building.

From the time Martin was first diagnosed with autism at about three-and-a-half-years-old, Joe and Colleen split their approaches and responsibilities for addressing Martin's disability. They decided Colleen would become a master of autism, because she was more interested in the science and research into treatments, and Joe would become a master of Martin, focusing on how and why they would apply different approaches to their son's autism.

Over the years they looked at all available treatments, everything from intense one-on-one therapy to supplements and other medications. They considered approaches available only in other states, knowing that taking advantage of the therapy would mean moving their family. They tried body movement therapy and auditory training to help Martin tolerate loud or sudden sounds, and they learned to prepare Martin for new experiences or difficult challenges through the use of social stories, building his vocabulary with word labels and pictures.

Music was an early hook into connecting Martin with the world around him because from an early age it was clear Martin perceived more than most people did in the music he heard. A second-grade teacher flagged their attention to Martin's connection with music, and Joe enlisted a musician friend who became Martin's piano teacher and also his friend. Although playing piano was more difficult for Martin, music theory came very easily to him, and he had perfect pitch.

Normal, everyday school interactions were difficult for Martin; there were many meltdowns and many years where Joe would get a call nearly every day about Martin's behavior.

As Martin got older, he experienced increasing difficulties understanding how other people saw him and understanding social rules and how to apply them. In middle school, Martin returned a boy's taunt with some choice words and gestures of his own—normal middle school response; but he did it right in front of a teacher—most middle schoolers would have waited until the teacher had turned their back. Martin got in trouble because he wasn't able to understand that he should change his behavior in front of adults the way the other kids did.

Martin went through the public schools, earning a modified diploma and continuing with independent living studies through the age of 21. Around that same time, Martin and his parents consulted a new doctor, one who offered them helpful new insight into Martin's disability and how to help him connect with the world around him.

The specialist helped them all see what could be perceived as Martin's arrogance was in fact a defense he had built up to help him avoid difficult circumstances and situations. Martin's thought processes are very linear, which can lead him to draw inaccurate conclusions from information. He also becomes easily distracted. The specialist also helped them see that Martin could learn complicated or difficult new systems if he was taught with tremendous repetition and patience. In addition, a new therapist helped Martin learn new ways to cope with frustration and regulate his emotions.

Things had gotten really rough between Martin and his dad in the teen years, but the new evaluation from the specialist and new approach from the therapist "allowed me back into his life," says Joe. It allowed him to learn how to better talk with Martin, slow down and work with him.

Although many marriages buckle under the pressure of a child with special needs, Joe says that Martin was never a threat to their marriage. "Certainly," says Joe, "at times we would get depressed, or frustrated, or afraid, but we never took it out on each other. Martin was never an issue that would have driven us apart. Martin was an adventure and a learning opportunity."

My mom is secretive.

She is not really my mom, she's a secret agent. Moms usually watch over you. Mine would spy. She planted a GPS device in my underwear.

We had a password for breakfast. My dad kept forgetting it. That's how he lost 20lbs.

Connecting through comedy

Comedy is all about connecting to an audience. You will not be funny if you can't connect with the audience, and yet connection had always been one of Martin's biggest challenges. Comedy has functioned as a transformative lens through which Martin can observe and engage the world around him, and then actually connect with people through humor.

Joe found out about SMH chatting with Dave Mowry at a local chamber of commerce event, and he asked Dave if Martin could participate, as Martin had always voiced the desire to be a comedian. Dave replied that Martin would be welcome, and they'd see if the classes would be comfortable for him. Neither Joe or Martin had qualms about Martin taking the class with folks with severe mental illness. Joe says that to him, it's all related. "Martin's disability is mental – it's in his brain."

Joe observed as we did that Martin was quiet and seemingly disengaged for the first few comedy classes, noting that Martin was quiet before and after the classes as well. But Martin was paying attention. "I know Martin was surprised he learned so much in the classes about telling a story or structuring a joke," Joe says. "I thought it was nice that it was such a supportive environment, since being in social situations and having to learn with others makes him anxious. He got some good ideas, and importantly he realized he could learn things from others and get along with them."

Joe notes that Martin's approach to humor is different. He studied what made a joke funny or not through the SMH classes, through Dave's coaching, and through reading books. He feels that Martin approaches comedy as if it were a math problem: If this setup, then divert to this unexpected punchline = big laugh!

Humor was a big part of family life for Martin, and in fact one of Joe's biggest joys in life is in cracking up his wife, Colleen, who is the "family laugher." Martin's younger brother is funny too, and so Martin had ample opportunity to watch funny happening in his own family.

This last Christmas break, Martin achieved the gold medal in sibling approval – he was finally able to crack up his younger brother, eliciting an honest-to-goodness belly laugh. In so doing, Martin was fitting right into his family's culture of laughter and love.

Martin plays in a local band of other musicians living with disabilities, and his stand-up experience also helped him onstage with the band, as he now is able to get up in front, make a few jokes onstage and talk. "I have," he confirms, "been known to make people laugh when performing with my band." Martin not only plays keyboard in the band, but he also does work for clients producing music charts with a complicated musical software program called Sibelius.

Though Martin is currently living with his parents, he is quite independent, and his folks are able to leave him in charge of the house for several days at a time. They have hopes that someday he will be living on his own, and they feel he is perfectly capable of it.

> *I've been banned from the movie theater.*
> *There was a problem with my food.*
> *The pizza delivery guy made too much noise.*

Like many SMH comedians, Martin's comedy is not just transformative for him, but for his audiences. Through the SMH classes and the performances, Martin went from being an oddball off to the side to center stage, connecting with the whole audience and individual audience members. Remember Martin's family friend Wilda? She succinctly summarizes Martin's comedy transformation. "That evening I saw Martin being comfortable in a room of people, and with himself in that room."

Because people put themselves out there both by performing stand-up and by being vulnerable responding to the humor there are deep lessons to be learned from comedy. Joe admires Martin's ability to reflect in his comedy who he is and what his strengths are. "The funniest comedians," says the proud dad, "strike a chord of truth similar to the best philosophers and social observers."

Now Martin wields the power of his experiences with autism to take the audience on a journey of laughter and understanding. If through that journey Martin is now more comfortable with himself and his place in this world, that's a win-win, because Martin is a pretty cool guy.

Let's finish with Martin on Martin.

Martin, on what he'd like people to know about him:

"I want people to know I like to joke around and just hang out. But there is more to me than telling jokes, I play keyboard and a little drums, and I've played a little basketball. As part of my disability, I notice a lot of things differently, including things about music."

Martin, to people with autism:

"Since I represent a group of disabilities – or special abilities, depending on how you think of it – I'm really a normal person, at least that's how I live. I understand that some people with autism go into their own little world, and I say that's ok. I think my disability is nothing. Often times I go into my own world, but I stay aware. It might come off as crazy to some people, but they don't know you. Like, sometimes people can hear me when I didn't mean for them to, or the opposite – they can't hear me when I intended to say something out loud.

"You can be too sensitive, or too oblivious. Being oblivious of what is going on around you can be good or bad depending on the situation … just a time not to be oblivious … say you're crossing the street. You don't want to get injured you know. I mean, sometimes I can lose my train of thought without even knowing it."

Martin, on being a stand-up comedian with a

disability:

"When you first meet a person you see their talent; you don't know they have a disability like me or bipolar like Dave. I guess I do consider myself a comedian. Since the video is on YouTube, yeah, I guess people who watch that will think of me first as a comedian."

Martin, on achieving his dream to do stand-up comedy:

"Well, at first it's just something you've always wanted to do, and then all of a sudden, you've done it. I was fulfilled, really, at a loss for words. It was the fulfillment of a dream I'd had on and off for as long as I can remember." Martin pauses here, reflecting, and pronounces dramatically that "it doesn't matter even if you've been waiting your whole life for it."

Then he quips dryly, with his typical sly smile, "Oh, don't write that, even I don't know what that means."

CHAPTER 4

TARA

Don't get me wrong. We love our family members who live with mental illness. Seriously, you inspire us. We want you to be happy, we want you to reach your full potential, and WE WANT YOU TO TAKE YOUR FREAKING MEDICATION!!
—Tara

When I'm performing with our mental health comedy group, I often joke that I am the token minority, the only comic in our little troupe who does not live with my own mental illness.

I live with and experience severe mental illness and have for the last several years. It just hasn't been my own! I am a family member, and I live with my loved ones' mental illness. To be sure, that has resulted in the occasional bout of situational depression and vicarious PTSD, but that's a common side effect for us family members.

I am aunt and advocate to three amazing young nieces who have experienced PTSD, depression, anxiety, and borderline personality disorder, with a little traumatic brain injury to spice things up. In walking alongside them I have found myself becoming a stand-up comedian and professional speaker, using humor to take power over chaos, increase the awareness of mental illness and break the stigma it still carries.

Boring in a really great way

Seriously, that's all you need to know about my childhood, college, and early adult years. Of course, that's not all I'm going to tell you because this is a book, not a postcard. But Boring in a Really Great Way does cover it.

I was raised in Wasilla, Alaska, where I could not see Russia, but I often did see members of one-time vice-presidential candidate Sarah Palin's family, all of whom are lovely. Quirky, maybe, but lovely. I realize now there were a few other peculiarities of being raised in Alaska, such as learning mad winter driving skills and believing as a kid that there was a moose in our dark scary basement instead of the requisite monster, but mostly my childhood was typical of being raised in a small town.

I was raised with a younger brother, Scott, and two teacher parents. Solid upper-middle class situation in a rural Alaskan town that grew rapidly more suburban throughout my childhood, providing the necessary accoutrements of fast-food restaurants and even a mall by the time my teenage years required it.

My folks were happily married for nearly 54 years, until my father's recent death. They were loving, strict and encouraging, and provided Scott and I a rich template of healthy marriage and family life centered around each other, our little Presbyterian church family, and our larger community. Now, having seen firsthand and close-up what a gaping, festering wound can result in the lives of children without that example, I am doubly grateful for what we had.

Scott and I were both pretty good kids. I was a serious, relatively nerdy girl, an academic overachiever headed for college who took dance lessons and wanted to grow up to be the next Oprah. Scott was a compassionate, faithful, artistic kid who was into Cub Scouts, Student Troopers, three-wheel ATV's and hunting and fishing with my dad. He had severe ADHD, a close pack of oddball friends and a penchant for reaching out to those who were hurting, serving as a deacon at our church by his early twenties.

So, what happened?

You may ask, then, *how in the heck* did my brother wind up with three baby girls and a wife who would leave him for a pedophile before he was in his late twenties? How did my Boringly Great Family wind up in an overly melodramatic saga of abuse and mental illness that would painfully and permanently alter our family's story?

My family now believes that as a young boy in elementary school, my brother either experienced or witnessed abuse by his adult Cub Scout leader, a man who was later convicted and sent to prison for child abuse. At the time this scandal was breaking publicly, my brother began showing significant signs of distress, washing his hands repeatedly or tapping walls in an obsessive-compulsive kind of way. Though my folks asked, my brother never shared or admitted to any abuse from his Scout leader. Looking back, it is clear something happened that was upsetting to him. Whatever this trauma may have been, I believe it set him up to be both more empathetic and more vulnerable to others later in his life.

When he was still a teenager, Scott met and began dating a much younger new member of our church's high school youth group, a funny, smart foster kid who was quite open about the abuse she had endured at the hands of her mother's boyfriends and others. *(In hindsight, I now recognize her inappropriate openness as a symptom of her abuse, of safe boundaries never allowed to form. In my ignorance at the time, I just thought it was weird.)* Even though their relationship was tumultuous, and it was clear to others around him that this girl was troubled, my brother was deeply in love and loyal to the core. After dating her on and off for several years, they married when she was 17 years old. She was also eight months pregnant.

Within a few years they had become parents of three little girls, and my brother had started his own taxicab business. His business grew, he continued to serve as a deacon in the church, and he was growing into the position of young local businessman, occasionally even discussing local business issues with Wasilla's mayor at the time, Sarah Palin. His marriage, however, was on the rocks, and in the fall of 1997 his wife left Scott for one of his best friends from high school, with whom she had been having an affair. This was the man who would become my nieces' stepfather and abuser. Of course, neither my brother or our family knew that at the time.

In the midst of the stress of the separation, pending divorce and looming custody battle that fall, Scott fell ill with influenza A and then pneumonia. He took the girls to their elementary school Halloween carnival on a Friday night, was hospitalized the next day and in a coma with adult respiratory distress syndrome by Sunday. He survived in the coma for about a month before ultimately passing away.

After his death, my nieces' mother left all three of the girls with my grieving parents, claiming the stress of parenthood was too much for her. But after about a year, she and her boyfriend reappeared, wanting to reclaim the girls, and my parents felt they had no legal or moral choice but to return the girls to the woman who was, after all, their mother.

My parents and I may always second guess that decision, occasionally allowing our minds to drift to "what if's" and "what could have been's." But the truth of the matter is that no normal, healthy person without prior knowledge could ever anticipate or predict the years of abuse and isolation that the girls would endure.

No one expects a pedophile

Most people live obliviously in a world where the baseline expectation is that adults do not hurt children, and they cannot expect or predict a pedophile. We had no awareness of or education about how her own childhood abuse might have affected the girls' biological mothers' adult parenting decisions or the likelihood that she would be able to act to keep the girls safe.

The girls spent the next several years with their mom and their stepdad, moving frequently, in and out of school. At first, they were allowed to visit my folks for a few weeks at a time in the summers, but eventually contact was restricted. When we asked, their mother wouldn't tell us where she was calling from, and letters arrived without return addresses. We often went months at a time without even knowing what state they were in.

This isolationist behavior was absolutely typical for an abuser, but while we had vague suspicions that the stepdad was "a bad guy," we did not recognize the danger signs for what they actually meant. My brother's youngest daughter, L[1] was removed from the home at the age of eight on vague accusations of abuse, and eventually relinquished to my parent's custody, a few years before the other girls got out, but it was some time before she was capable of sharing any details of abuse with them.

This is typical of abuse situations. Even the most horribly abused children often love their parents, want their parent's approval, and seek to protect their parents. Not only that, but much of what they experience seems normal to them, including missing school, neglect, and being tasked with inappropriate parenting responsibilities for siblings. Two years before Scott's youngest daughter was taken from the home, the family had been joined by a baby sister, a baby girl who would

---

1 Names have been omitted for my nieces' *safety, privacy, and protection.*

essentially be raised by her sisters, still children themselves.

In December 2007, the girls' mother brought the other girls to the Portland area where my husband and I live for a short visit with us, the first we'd seen of them in an exceptionally long time. My parents were in town from Alaska with L, who at that point was 12 years old. We exchanged Christmas presents, went ice skating at the local mall, and tried to reestablish relationships with the girls, who were 15, 14 and 5. It was a relatively pleasant visit, with no hint of what was about to come.

(At the time their mom, unbeknownst to us, was living in a different state than the girls. She and the stepdad had separated many times over the years, in part due to domestic violence and her twisted jealousy over his sexual abuse of her children. At some point she had become fully aware of the sexual, physical, and emotional abuse her daughters were experiencing, yet when she left, she nearly always left the girls with him. We knew nothing of these separations until years later.)

Barely three weeks after that Christmas visit, in January 2008, the girls' stepdad asked my oldest niece, C, to drive and pick up her two younger sisters from school. She was an unlicensed 15-year-old, and she pulled out on the rural highway in front of an older gentleman and was t-boned by his vehicle. C was not wearing a seat belt, and on impact she catapulted through the front windshield of the pick-up truck, striking her head on the pavement 40 feet away.

Immediately after her accident, C was tenuously stabilized at the local hospital and then life-flighted to Portland, where she would spend the next several weeks in a coma. The girls' mother, two states away from where her daughters were living, had called my mom, who called me. After frantic calls to several local hospitals, I finally found C at Doernbecher Children's Hospital. I will never forget the sober tones of the social worker they called to the phone. She told me that even though I was not immediate family – and therefore not normally allowed – that I should "just get here, as fast as you can," as C's chances of survival were so slim. Indeed, nurses later told me that they had not expected C to survive, and then not expected her to ever leave a vegetative state.

I was the first and only family member at the hospital, and I stayed by her side until her mother called from the road and ordered me to leave. She had gone to meet the stepdad in eastern Oregon, and they were driving to Portland together. They were still a couple of hours away, but she demanded that I leave well before they arrived, because "he did not want to see" me. Even in this life-or-death situation, childhood abuse had warped her own maternal responses. Protecting the abuser trumped all, despite the fact that her daughter could have died alone before they got there.

The car accident, with the ensuing stress and turmoil, was a catalyst that set into motion the events that would free the girls from their abusers. My brother's middle daughter, K, was able to summon the superhuman courage required to report her stepfather's abuse to the authorities. Within a couple of days, the remaining two girls, K and her youngest sister, were removed from their home and put into foster care, and their abuser was arrested. He would be tried and convicted that

June, largely by his own words written in his journals, and is currently serving a sentence of thirty years with no chance of parole. *(The sentence is not, and could not, be long enough to make up for the damage his abuse has caused throughout our family, and in the girls' lives.)*

K and her youngest sister were initially placed in foster care in their rural eastern Oregon community. Unfortunately, it became clear that the girls weren't safe staying there in a town full of family members and friends who continued to support their abusers, and even blamed K for her courageous reporting. It was at that point that DHS asked my husband and I to step in as foster parents, and the two girls came to our home that same June.

C remained in the hospital for several months, recovering from the coma, broken bones and a severe brain injury incurred in the accident, and then transitioned into specialized medical foster care. L remained with my parents.

If you suspect or are aware of child abuse:

- **Report it.** Call 911, call your local child protective services agency, and/or call the child's school. Tell someone. That child may have no one but you to stand in the gap for them and protect them.
- **Don't think someone else will do it.** The situation may be such that it will require multiple sources of verification and inquiry to get the child to safety. Keep fighting. Abuse thrives in darkness and isolation.

It's been hard, for sure.

There have been days when we were so deep in crises, and I felt so powerless, that all I could do was go into a public bathroom and repeatedly wave my hands in front of the paper towel machine.

Finally, something I could control!

My journey as a family member of those living with mental illness has included two transformations. The first transformation took me from knowing very little about mental illness to the reality of walking alongside a teenager in the deepest darkest throes of depression, anxiety, severe PTSD and intense suicidality. The second was the surprising amount of personal growth required of me to be effective in walking alongside those teenagers, now young adults, on their journeys. This personal growth was capped off by my equally surprising new-found love of and talent for stand-up comedy.

How dumb were we?

We took two of our nieces, K and the youngest sister, into our home as foster kids in late spring 2008. *(C, the oldest, was still in the hospital, and L was with my folks. I know, it gets confusing.)* Between the day we made the decision to be foster parents and the day a couple of weeks later when we were able to actually pick the girls up from a distant community across the state, we learned that K, the older of the two girls, had already made one suicide attempt and had also been cutting. (Until the phone call from the social worker telling me about it, I'd never even heard of cutting. Bless my clueless heart.) The story of what they'd been through had filled out, and it was a story of truly horrific abuse and neglect.

Despite everything they'd been through, we genuinely believed back then that if we loved the girls, housed them, provided them with all the material things they'd lacked, the experiences they'd never had, and modeled a "good" family life, they would be ok. Because we would LOVE them.

Boy, were we dumb.

So, so dumb.

It's OK for those of you with any knowledge about foster parenting or the effects of severe childhood abuse to go ahead and laugh. Go ahead. The rest of us will wait. In retrospect, it is pretty funny, in a "holy crap why didn't someone tell us what we were getting ourselves into" kind of way.

We had no idea how naive we were, of course, and, in fact, the girls were with us for an entire summer before we even took the required training from DHS that could have provided us some basic perspective. We were busy that summer getting the girls caught up on medical, dental, and psychiatric appointments, plus just getting our new family of seven acclimated to each other.

The foster-parenting training dates didn't work with our schedule for the summer, and I believe DHS was so happy to have a decent family for the girls that they were all too willing to let us wait for fall. Unfortunately, what that meant was that we had completely exhausted the standard honeymoon season of any new foster parenting placement before we got a tiny, tiny clue.

I don't really blame DHS for our poor preparation, as the

girls' abuse and their initial foster placements all took place in a community that had been completely decimated by the methamphetamine epidemic, where law enforcement and social services were overwhelmed and understaffed.

My husband and I, what with our upper-middle class professional lives, college educations and tight family and church support networks, must have seemed like an easy slam-dunk to the caseworkers. So, if they knew how completely ignorant, woefully unprepared, or dreadfully clueless we were, they probably flinched a little at my Pollyanna-esque naiveté and forced themselves to move on to the next family in need.

That first summer with the two girls in our home was a whirlwind of activity. I felt compelled to fill their days with fun, joy, and healthy family activities. Not only that, but I was overcompensating a bit for my own three little boys, figuring MORE FUN would help make up for having to share mommy, daddy, and their home space.

My boys were 7-, 5-, and 2-years-old at the time, and we kept things simple for them. We told them the girls' parents had a lot of problems and had made some bad choices *(Hello …UNDERSTATEMENT)* and they couldn't take care of the girls. The boys accepted it all without much question. There was plenty of excitement to distract them, from remodeling our family room downstairs by splitting it to add an additional bedroom for the girls, to the novelty of having girls, including a 14-year-old girl – a teenager – around all the time.

We began our foster-parenting training that fall. We had only been in class for a couple of weeks when K was first hospitalized for suicidal thoughts. Our trainer was a godsend, allowing me to vent and question and share more horrible details of K's rapid continuing decompensation, her self-harm attempts, her auditory and visual hallucinations. The trainer was honest, she was real, and she was the perfect mix of sympathetic and "Buck Up, Sister, it's going to be a bumpy ride!"

And boy, did K decompensate. I believe that once she had the assurance that her baby sister – whom she had helped raise – was safe with us, she let down the brittle walls she'd built to allow herself to function, walls she had created to stay outwardly sane and ensure her own and her baby sister's safety.

Mental illness myth: *Hearing voices or seeing things that aren't there automatically = schizophrenia.*

Truth: *There are many types of mental illness that manifest auditory or visual hallucinations, including PTSD, bipolar disorder, schizo-affective disorder, and others.*

That hospitalization was the first of many stays in the psych unit. K would spend most of the next three years in the hospital or in residential mental health treatment facilities, interspersed with only brief attempts to live in the community, either in our home or in other foster homes.

How awful DID things get? Well, there was the day that both of my parents were having surgery in the same hospital – one planned, one emergency. K chose that day to run away, on her bike and on the bus, and then got really angry at ME when I shared enough of her history with the police to hopefully prevent them from triggering her or employing unnecessary roughness. I spent the day moving between surgical waiting rooms on two different floors of the hospital, stepping out, talking to police, stepping back in and talking to my parents and their doctors, stepping out and talking to K. That was a bad day.

There were many that were worse.

That same fall, L, who had been living with my parents, also wound up in the hospital due to severe PTSD, and she began what would be almost four years of residential treatment. Keep in mind that it is unusual for children and teenagers to receive more than a few months in a residential treatment facility due to insurance restrictions and concerns about the institutionalizing effects of long-term residential treatment. The long periods of treatment my nieces received speaks both to the severity of their abuse and its effects, as well as the generosity of the state-funded care they received as foster children, for which we will always be grateful. I have no question that without that care, neither K or L would have survived their teen years.

The oldest girl, C, improved after recovering from her car accident and coma, and moved from medical foster care into a group home for adults with disability. She will always have some cognitive and memory issues, and I am now her legal guardian.

Their youngest sister lived with us in our home for a full year until DHS terminated her biological mother's rights and found her a wonderful adoptive family in our community.

What NOT to say to a person living with mental

illness *(or, Learn from my ignorance)*

I have specific memories of walking through our neighborhood with my niece K, not long after she moved in with us. She patiently explained to me that when she was suicidal, it didn't help for me to keep asking her "Are you suicidal now? Are you suicidal now? How about now? Do you wanna kill yourself now?" like I was some awful version of the guy in the ubiquitous cell-phone ads.

Shockingly, those types of questions were apparently not helpful. It would be the first of many times she would have to help me help her, even in the midst of her own mental anguish.

According to Mental Health First Aid training, it only takes one person walking alongside someone in a mental health crisis to make a difference. It was certainly true for K. There was more than one occasion in which K didn't try to kill herself simply because one person in her life – a teacher, a counselor, a friend – had simply made her promise not to do it that day or made her promise to see them the next day.

When K was intensely suicidal, it seemed the most banal thing would be enough to stave off or avert a suicide attempt – a promise to call a friend, being too sleepy from her nighttime meds to wake up to the alarm she set for the planned middle of the night attempt, or having completed homework she needed to turn in to a teacher.

As much as she desperately just wanted her pain to end, she continued to bravely reach out and grasp anything she could cling to in order to get through the next day, or the next hours. I will never know how much courage it took for her to go on until things got better, but I know I will be forever grateful.

It helped that K is and always has been a people pleaser. "I **would** kill myself, but darn it I promised my teacher I'd turn in that English paper tomorrow," was honestly sometimes her line of thinking. She didn't want to upset or disappoint anyone, even though she was in such pain that she wanted to die, or at least cease existing.

There have been a few amazing women that intersected with K early on – her junior high guidance counselor, her first foster mom, her first boyfriend's mom *(who she and we now consider her real mom)* – who have served as vital touchstones for her in her worst moments.

Why am I not in that list? Or her grandparents?

Well, at times over the past several years we have been, now and again. But a really unfortunate, tragic facet of the girls' early lives was the near-complete brainwashing they received from their abusive parent and stepparent regarding us, their paternal biological family. They were told over and over again that we were bad people; that we would get their parents in trouble; that we would call the police and have the kids taken away. They were also consciously encouraged to forget their biological father and told to call the new guy "Dad" right away, even before my brother had died.

Abuse results in many secondary victims. The girls have suffered exponentially greater losses and injuries, but nonetheless, the loss of our natural family relationships and the irreversible damage done to those relationships is just one of the many very real harms directly to my parents and me caused by their abusers. Because of the isolating, twisted manipulations of their mother and stepdad, we may never have with my nieces the close trusting relationships we were meant to have.

This brainwashing resulted in serious mental dissonance, especially for K, once she and her youngest sister had daily contact with us living in our home. K observed clearly over time that we were kind, we weren't "out to get her" or her sisters, and we weren't, in fact, the Bogeymen we'd been made out to be. However, those observations clearly contradicted the information that she had been fed by those closest to her, those whom naturally and inherently she had believed to be good and truthful. This kind of contradictory information is very hard for kids to decipher and is one reason we always tried *(not always succeeded, mind you, but oh, we tried)* to be very factual about both their biological mother and their stepdad, without including our emotions and judgment. We didn't want to add to their confusion and pain.

Thus, our relationship continues to evolve. We continue to bump up against issues triggered by those earliest statements made to the girls about us. In those bumpy moments, the girls often flip back to not trusting us, not believing we want good for them, or not believing that we care. My parents and I have had to press forward knowing that often those voices from childhood ring more loudly in their hearts and minds than the deep love we feel for each of them every day.

Through my research, training as a family advocate, and my education as a foster parent, I have learned that chronic childhood abuse – whether physical, sexual, or emotional – can cause permanent, disabling biological injury to the brain on a par with the traumatic brain injury that C, my oldest niece, lives with from her near fatal car crash. As I've worked with many other students in the SMH comedy classes and met other people through NAMI, it has become clear to me that this world would have significantly fewer people living with mental illness if we could effectively stop big people from hurting little people.

What do you mean, I'm in charge of my feelings?

One of the hardest things I've had to confront as a family member is how much I needed to change and grow to be effective for the girls. My run-of-the-mill emotional regulation skills were working just fine in my daily life before we took in the girls. Not that I'd ever considered it, but if I had, I would have assumed those skills would continue to serve me just fine, thank you very much. After all, I was a professional, educated and competent, and I could handle the tough stuff.

Wrong. In fact, my emotional regulation skills were not adequate to the job of foster-parenting abused children with attachment issues. This was primarily true of my interactions with K. Sure, her baby sister had some emotional struggles and behavioral issues in the year she lived with us, but they primarily presented as long tantrums and crying jags at bedtime. Holding her close and assuring her she was safe and loved was both in my skill set and appropriate.

Parenting a self-harming, suicidal teenager with a serious truth-telling problem, however, was WAY outside my skill set. When the woman who would become K's primary therapist told me I needed to get a hold of myself because I was exacerbating the situation, I wasn't just embarrassed, I was furious! ***How dare she??!!***

Unfortunately, she was right. In the beginning, *I frequently made things worse* because my own anxiety, my own fears and worries, and my own preconceptions prevented me from being effective or helpful.

Of course, I could not admit that at the time. How dare she!! Did she not know how difficult this was? How terrifying this was? She didn't even have kids, how could she understand how it felt to go to sleep, not knowing if K would sneak out in the middle of the night to try and kill herself again. How could she know how it felt, not knowing each night if we would be awakened AGAIN by the shrill ring of the phone, or another knock on the door from a police officer with concern and sympathy in their eyes.

Turns out, it wasn't really that important whether she'd had kids, or whether she was sympathetic enough to me and what we were going through. She was highly skilled in working with kids like K, and she was calm, reassuring, and effective ... with K. That was what mattered. But meanwhile, I had to take a deep breath or nine, and begin to think about what the therapist had said.

I had always operated under the comforting belief system that my feelings *(which in my case should always be referred to as Feelings, or possibly FEELINGS)*, WERE me and happened TO me. My husband and I would joke about how I was just ONE BIG FEELING that he accidentally ran into occasionally. I believed my feelings were externally caused, out of my control, and that I could not be held accountable for them. I certainly couldn't consciously change them or affect their intensity.

Convenient thinking for sure, but not true or effective, as I would painfully discover.

'Cause as family members, we just have different skill sets, right?

Other parents know the best dance studio or the best soccer coach.

I can give you a tour of all the ER waiting rooms and psych units in the greater Portland area and point out the best restrooms and vending machines!

Reshaping expectations: so many lessons

Other lessons I learned as a family member included the surprising truth that I COULD adapt to a new reality that would have seemed completely bonkers before mental illness entered our family members' lives. There were times when a month or a week without a run-away situation or a suicide attempt was all we could hope for. Three months without either was cause for great relief. Of course, the whole time I would have a growing sense of dread, convinced from experience that the other shoe was always about to drop. As a family member of a person living with mental illness, it is not uncommon to develop your own legitimate symptoms of PTSD, as you find yourself constantly on alert, hypervigilant for the next crisis. It's exhausting.

Another lesson from parenting or foster-parenting a teen

with mental illness is that you must release all pre-conceived expectations of parenting. Success must be completely and frequently redrawn and redefined.

I unfortunately took a LONG time to achieve this more open approach to what would define success for K. *(Yes, now I realize the inherent irony of even assuming it was my job to forecast her success. I can only hope my own boys receive some benefit from these "aha!" lessons I've learned.)* I sat through more than one team meeting that first year or two with therapists, the insurance care coordinator, DHS caseworker, schoolteachers, and administrators, verbally agonizing about K's class choices and options, her class credit situation, and her progress toward graduation. Meanwhile every other team member, including K, would stare at me in disbelief, as if I were fretting about damage to a car's paint job when the car was hurtling the wrong way down a packed highway, striking every car in its path while heading directly for a brick wall, with no available brakes.

I have no doubt that my innocently self-satisfied, yuppie-esque confidence in my own life, in my educational and professional choices absolutely complicated my ability to see other ways forward for K. I came to my foster parenting duties with the same set of preconceived values and expectations that my parents had for me, and that I hold for my own children. *(Or that I will hopefully now hold loosely for my boys, while being more aware of whether they consider them to be the appropriate expectations for THEM.)*

In my defense, letting go of the "normal" parental expectations with which I had been raised was complicated, since my own kids were little at the time, and I'd had no experience with teenagers. Not only that, but K is a particularly bright, creative, and competent person when she is not in the midst of a mental health crisis, and often even when she is. Under the parameters I knew, K should have been aiming to finish a competitive high school program and apply for college as the end goal. It took me quite some time to realize that while I was stressed out about whether her science credits would be adequate, everyone else was desperately seeking ways to move K forward slowly and safely while most importantly KEEPING HER ALIVE.

When my expectations were held up in the light of K's unstable mental health, and her childhood of severe abuse, poverty, and neglect, they were revealed to be patently ridiculous. Everyone else involved saw that long before I did. Learning to accept that – to live in the moment with her and build expectations based on where she was at the time and what she was capable of in that moment – was excruciatingly difficult.

There are times it might be easier to homeschool than parent in this competitive environment. Yesterday was the last day of teacher appreciation week, which is out of control. We had to bring flowers one day, write notes another day, bake a treat, make a meal, do their laundry.

Teachers are GREAT but it's too much. I'm just waiting for "Present a Poem Hand-Knit onto a Shawl Woven from the Wool of Baby Llamas Raised on the Sweet Blossoms of Organic Buttercups Day."

DBT for everyone!

Much of the credit for my eventual parenting transformation, such as it has been, must go to my TWO *(not that I'm counting) (or bitter)* trips through a mandatory 16-week course for parents of teens going through dialectical behavioral therapy (DBT) treatment. K had a set-back part way through my first round of the parent course and had to re-enter residential treatment, but I knew I'd need the skills when she came back home, so I stuck it out. Only to find out when she did come back out that I still had to accompany her through the entire program a second time. *(Or maybe the therapists just knew I needed serious extra help!)*

Turns out the skills K was learning in DBT, and I had to learn alongside her in the parent skills class, would be invaluable to both of us. Many of the emotional regulation skills K needed to develop so she had effective tools to handle overwhelming feelings of despair or anxiety were the same skills I needed to handle my anxiety about her illness, her self-harm attempts, and the resulting chaos and constant crisis.

The DBT parent course was taught in modules of four weeks, and admitted new members once every couple of months, which meant that new parents always found themselves in class alongside parents who had already been through much of the course, and who were further along in their learning and parenting.

When I began the parenting course, I was horrified, aghast to hear from other parents who were cheering their child's "achievement" of making it to their high school classes three of five days that week *(!)*, or "only" coming home drunk once in the last week, or "only" taking the car once without permission and staying out overnight without letting their parents know where they were.

The other parents seemed like normal people, well-intentioned parents who cared about their children, but I could not believe what low bars of achievement they were setting, and what low expectations they had for their AWFUL children. *(Ahh, blissfully ignorant arrogance, the best kind of arrogance.)*

Clearly these well-intentioned folks were horrible parents, and I had no place with them. If having my rear end planted in those chairs each week had not been required for K to access therapy at the clinic, I definitely would have hightailed it out of the first week at warp speed, never to return. *(Of course, if I'd known then what I know now, that at the time K was regularly subverting our alarm system and sneaking out after we were asleep to take public transit from our little suburb into downtown Portland to go clubbing with strangers, I might have been a wee bit less judgy.)*

I also would have missed the incredibly effective, perspective-changing lessons which have helped me parent K and my own kids and reshape my own emotional regulation to the benefit of my own life and relationships.

Always talking about self-care, it's so important for family members.

We are caregivers, so we have to take care of ourselves.

But it's hard. Along with the sharps, I had to lock up the alcohol and narcotics – how do I self-medicate?

Stress eating can only get me so far, people.

Isolation

In my experience, one of the toughest parts of parenting a child or teen with mental illness is the isolating nature of the struggles you face on a daily basis. The other moms at soccer practice or the playground are worried because little Jimmy is having a hard time learning fractions. You're worried because you just found a random stash of pills in your teenager's room — some prescribed and not taken, and some unfamiliar and definitely not prescribed — and you know it's a stash for a future overdose attempt, but you don't know if you should tell your kid you found and flushed them or just let her wonder what happened to them.

My daily worries were so different, filled with drama, fear, and pain, that I often felt isolated from the other moms in my circle. That isolation only intensified if I did share a tiny peek into my real-life terrors, because if Jimmy's mom found out about the self-harming and pill stashing, then she felt a bit awkward angsting about Jimmy's progress in fractions, and conversations died an awkward death.

I desperately needed two very disparate things: I needed folks in whom I could confide about the worst things that were happening without fear they would judge my girls or run from my pain and anxiety; and I needed *(ideally, but not necessarily, the same)* folks to be normal with me. For the love of Pete, please talk to me about fractions, about naughty back talk, and potty training!

I needed to know that the normal world in which I'd previously been parenting still existed. I wanted to cling to those moments of normalcy like a rat on a sinking life raft, moments that could give me hope that I might get to live in that world again. Those moments also served as a good reminder that I still had other kids, and that no matter how tired, sad, or overwhelmed I felt, I needed to be as "normal" a mom as possible for them.

I needed to stand alongside my mom friends as they worried about their child's understanding of fractions, or about their child's naughty outbursts, and their potty-training journey, because they deserved no less and I would not get those moments back.

Oh, how I needed and was desperately grateful for other moms to talk to me about my little boys, to comment, to reconnect me with their everyday as their mom. Not an easy thing to do when you have a teenager in the psych unit bent on self-destruction, or a younger girl who cries herself to sleep every night and tantrums for hours on end.

When dealing with a family member with severe mental illness, the urgent can all too easily become the everyday, and the everyday can all too easily be swept aside or ignored, moments never to be regained.

Thankfully, I have three healthy, bright, and well-adjusted kids who will hopefully not suffer any permanent negative effects from how tired, distracted, sad and, honestly, cranky I was for a long time.

Thankfully parenting a kid with mental illness is a great defensive weapon:
   Oh, no, you and Billy go ahead, we got stuff too.
   We have to go to the psychiatrist, therapy, then group

therapy, then I gotta go by the Rite-Aid and pick up the trazodone, Cymbalta, Prazosin, Saphris, and the Seroquel and then I got to go home and lock up the knives and scissors!

Parenting siblings of those with mental illness

I am counting on any ill effects my kids might have experienced from the chaos of their cousins' mental illness to be counterbalanced by the benefits of a deeper compassion for their cousins, a deeper understanding of how our faith has guided our response to love the girls sacrificially, and a "no big deal" straight-forward acceptance of mental health struggles.

They have grown up aware of their cousins' hospitalizations for mental illness the same as their grandparents' hospitalizations for joint replacement or pneumonia. They visited the girls with me in both the hospital and in various residential treatment facilities, bringing fast-food treats and board games, hanging out, and bringing a welcome distraction to the girls in their difficult daily lives as they worked to get better.

It wasn't until I was well into preparations to write this book with my co-author Dave that my husband and I gave them any specifics about their cousins' mental illness. They had been so young when the girls came into our home that we told them simply that the girls had experienced difficult things with parents who could not take care of them and they had to leave their families. That these hard things broke their brains a little bit and that they would get extra sad, and they would need help to feel better.

For a long time, this was all the information they needed, but when we began the Kickstarter campaign to fund this book, we knew the time had come to give them more specific information. Since it was going to happen on the Internet, my kids were automatically fascinated by the campaign, and we knew we needed to give them additional information and help them understand it.

This was confirmed for me when my 7-year-old asked if I would tell him some of my "jokes," and my 13-year-old jumped in and hurriedly said "oh, no, she can't, they're grown-up jokes." The boys had never heard my stand-up routine because I refer to things like hospitalizations, suicide attempts, self-harm, and medications. But I realized that my oldest thought I was telling dirty jokes, or jokes with bad words in them, because that's how we describe that kind of content when we are restricting them from seeing something! It was definitely time to clear the air. *(And no, I still didn't let the youngest hear my comedy, but I would let the other two if they asked, as long as there was a LOT of time afterward for Q & A.)*

They weren't easy conversations. Nobody wants to have to define the word suicide to their 7-year-old.

Their cousins' mental illness will likely continue to be a reality for my boys in their future, even into adulthood. Better that we are talking about it openly as a family now, so they have plenty of time to watch and absorb how my husband and I talk about it, how we approach it as a family, and how it factors into our relationships with their cousins.

I used to work in nonprofit management. But my husband and I have three kids of our own, so when I am not taking care of my nieces, I'm a stay-at-home mom. Not the homeschooling kind of stay-at-home mom, and

DEFINITELY not the homeschooling-while-raising-chickens-and-reupholstering-the-couch kind of stay-at-home mom, God bless'em.

I can't get my kids to flush consistently, let alone be responsible for their knowledge of participles.

Why didn't I ever get my own, REAL, therapy?

Who has the time? I sure didn't, parenting between three and five kids depending on the month, maintaining some semblance of a household *(not my strong suit on a good day)*, and interacting with school officials, therapists, social workers, and law enforcement, depending on the week.

We spent so much time in crisis after crisis–and I mean truly life-threatening crisis–that I didn't have the time to spend taking care of myself. Does that make it OK?

Absolutely not, and I don't recommend that excuse at all! Much as it drives me nuts to hear about self-care, it is critically important. If you burn out, get sick or break down, your family member may have no one left to count on. Good self-care not only helps prevent you from burning out but protects you against the dangers of isolation as a family member.

I did have several saving graces that many folks caring for family members with mental illness are not so lucky to have. I had, and am grateful to have, an unbelievably deep support network. In addition to my extremely supportive husband, I belong to a vibrant and caring church family, and have pastors who have known about and prayed for our journey.

We live in a very tight-knit little neighborhood, with

neighbors who knew just enough, demanded no more and did not pass judgment. There have been a few moms at the kids' school with whom I felt safe, and with whom I could connect with on the playground after school, honestly and transparently. About a year after the girls were put in foster care, my parents left their hometown of Wasilla, Alaska, where they had lived for more than forty years and moved to Oregon to be near my family so we could walk alongside the girls together.

Perhaps most importantly, I am a member of a small group of women in my church family who have met weekly for almost 11 years to grow in our faith, study, and support each other through listening, hugging and prayer. Whenever my heart was broken by some new detail of the girls' past, or the latest suicide attempt or run, these ladies listened, they let me monopolize our time on occasion, they loved me enough to tell me when I was off-base or when I should push harder, and then they allowed me to share in their everyday lives, their concerns about their kids and marriages and health crises and job crises. Without them, I would have absolutely had my own personal insider's view of the local psych units, and I am eternally grateful to them.

Finding that type of support is so important, because as a family member of someone living with mental illness you can feel so completely separated from the rest of your peers, from other families, and from society itself. As a family member's mental illness is often a chronic situation, you can be afraid that people will get tired of hearing about it, but on the other hand you feel fake and dishonest if you don't have the opportunity to go deeper than "everything's fine, thanks for asking."

Plus, I've found if you say "everything's fine, thanks" while sobbing or twitching uncontrollably, it can send confusing signals.

Another key source of support over the last six years has been the many conversations with K's therapists, conversations that walked the fine line of *(always)* respecting her confidentiality while giving me support and guidance with how to best handle events, parenting choices and decisions, and emotional support and encouragement – in the vein of yes, this is really hard, and you are a great mom/aunt/advocate. Often hearing those types of affirmations from the therapists, even when it seemed like they were reading from a script they were "supposed" to use with parents, was so helpful, especially on days when the situation seemed deeply hopeless, or when I felt like a giant failure.

These conversations varied in depth and frequency depending on the therapist and their approach to working with parents. Some therapists, especially early on, would share with me what they were working on and what obstacles were coming up with K. Some therapists, especially those who were more deeply identified with DBT, would barely speak to me at all without K present, and even then, only about things that they had already decided together to discuss with me.

This of course was occasionally very frustrating for me, as I wanted to know what was going on, how therapy was progressing, and what I could be doing at home to support the therapeutic process.

I did find that even the most close-lipped therapists were usually willing to listen to me, even if they could not respond out of respect for confidentiality and/or the patient/therapist relationship. So, if I found a new stash of hidden pills, or if I was concerned about self-harm or other safety issues, they would often listen and consider it before their next conversation with K.

The other critical component for me has been my Christian faith, which has deepened as I have experienced the undeserved and overflowing grace of God's love. I have been reminded over and over that on paper, our girls should be dead, living on the street or as victims of new abusers. Over and over, we have experienced God's hand protecting the girls in otherwise hopeless situations, encouraging, and upholding us in our darkest moments, and assuring us that we and the girls are loved by Him.

Even with all of my "natural" supports, as the above are sometimes termed, looking back I know there have been times when I should have gotten more direct help, times where dumping everything on a professional would have been a good thing. Honestly, at times it has been too much, too ugly, and too painful, and probably was really more than my husband, my friends and family should have had to carry with me without professional help.

What we really need is for society to have a more accepting view of the mental health spectrum!

We need to wield the most powerful force for change in American culture—TV.

You've heard of the show "Portlandia?"

We'd have a show called "Schizophrenia." Or

"Bipolaria" —it would be perfect!

The show about PTSD would be the worst, though, it's always in flashbacks ... reruns.

Me, a comedian?

A few years into our journey, at a time when K was safely ensconced in residential treatment and her littlest sister was with her new adoptive family, I was able to return to part-time work. I made a career switch from nonprofit management and took a part-time position as a peer support specialist, working with other families with kids living with mental illness in a great organization called the Oregon Family Support Network (OFSN). It was in the course of my work with OFSN that I met Dave Mowry, my co-author. Dave and I were both taking an intensive peer support training that involved a lot of role playing, skit work, and other open sharing of the class lessons. Dave, who was working through the Stand Up for Mental Health class for the second time, invited me to join the comedy class.

After Dave talked to me about the class, he brought me a copy of the workbook they'd been working through from Dave Granirer. Then Dave said they had a performance coming up in a couple of weeks at a fundraiser for their local NAMI chapter, and if I was able to come up with a few minutes of material they'd be happy to have me perform with them.

I was just about to leave for a two-week spring break family vacation to Arizona to visit my mother-in-law, so I thanked Dave for the workbook and the invitation but warned him it was unlikely to happen.

I read the workbook on the plane, and ideas began to percolate immediately. Once we arrived in Arizona, I sat down in the first quiet moment, and the material began to pour forcefully out of me, as if a faucet under great pressure had been released. I've rarely had such a fluid creative experience, and in fact most of the material was coming out fully or almost fully formed, needing only slight tweaking.

Putting it down on paper was exhilarating and validating all at once, and I could hear exactly the way I would perform each joke in my head as I wrote it.

I told almost no one about that first performance, and I was definitely glad no one in the audience was likely to know me, but as my time on stage approached, I got more and more excited.

I wasn't particularly nervous about being on stage in front of folks, as I have done a great deal of public speaking throughout my career. I have always loved being on stage, and I've always loved performing. Until comedy, I just hadn't had any particular skills or talent to justify it!

Finding out I have a talent for stand-up has been like finally finding that one rhomboid-shaped piece to fit in a rhomboid-shaped hole in my life that I wasn't even aware existed.

Performing the first time was both as exhilarating and confirming as writing the material had been, and it's really been the same with every performance. It's as if onstage I hear a loud, satisfying click, and everything falls into place and I know that THIS is where I'm supposed to be. Since then, I helped Dave facilitate classes in Clackamas County, coaching student comics and helping them write their jokes, as well as performing with Dave around the area.

That first performance and those that followed allowed me something I'd not permitted myself to do before: own my journey. Before stand-up, I felt very much that the journey we were on with the girls, though the right thing to do, was also the only thing I could do.

It felt like it was happening to me, to my parents, to my marriage, to my kids, and it was out of my control. Not only that, but it was so clear that we were making the journey with so much more than so many do. I had a great education; previous jobs meant I was confident and comfortable with medical professionals; I had a tight knit fully supportive family and a small group of girlfriends who prayed us through every obstacle, every bump in the road and every crisis. No matter how awful things got, it seemed like it was my duty, I just had to keep soldiering on. Plus, we were "just" the helpers, so spending time mourning the sacrifices we'd made, grieving the losses our whole family had experienced as a result of the abusers, or being sad about any of it for more than a few minutes felt incredibly selfish, especially when the girls were fighting the darkness for their very lives every day.

Comedy allowed me to finally OWN this journey for myself, to claim my pain and my truth. My experiences, my grief, and my feelings count. With comedy I have a therapeutic and appropriate venue through which I can speak my truth. It is a way I can boldly and unapologetically say–without feeling maudlin or selfish–that at times this journey has been horrifically difficult, painful, and lonely.

There have been awful moments of fear and sadness that

no one should have to experience, and times when I shook with anger – anger at the abusers who hurt our girls so deeply, anger at the shortcomings of the system, anger at the disordered thinking and inconsiderate behavior of the teenager in question at the moment, or anger at the little stupidities that threatened at times to be the straw on the proverbial camel's back.

In the beauty that is the connectedness of the human experience, when I speak my truth, I get to either open your eyes, illuminate a portion of your journey for you to see through a new lens, or illuminate that journey for others. *(This more than makes up for the fact that I never saw myself as a person who would say something so melodramatic as "I can speak my truth." Eh, it is what it is.)*

I find tremendous freedom and validation in getting to BE angry, sarcastic, and pointedly, wickedly, funny about these truths while still making people laugh.

Having a parent, a spouse or a sibling come up to me after a show with tears in their eyes, saying "How did you know?" and thanking me for sharing their story, their pain, their frustration, and hopelessness? Glorious frosting on the cake, and balm to my do-gooder advocate's heart.

Many family members are too exhausted, too hopeless, and/or too mired in the day-to-day survival of their loved one's mental illness to be able to share or speak up in this way, and whenever I think about it, I am convicted again of the beautiful gift I've found in stand-up comedy.

As a family member, you gotta have their back, you got-ta be alert. You can't always count on the professionals, like residential staff when a teen is really self-harming.

Once (OK, three times) my niece was rushed from a residential facility to the ER because she'd swallowed a pencil. On her return?

"Oh, honey, you swallowed a pencil. Here, we'd like you to process what you were feeling, journal about that … here's a notebook and A PENCIL." Three times!!! Seriously?

Being funny about the awful

Some parts of our experience have been too powerful, too horrible or too personal to the girls to turn into comedy, or to share here in this book. Figuring out where that line is and maximizing the humor of every moment is definitely an exercise of skill and audience judgment. For crowds with significant experience or familiarity with mental illness, I tell one joke about how the staff of a residential treatment center let one of my nieces repeatedly swallow a pencil when she was particularly self-harming.

That joke is tough to share with a general crowd, as it shines an instantaneous light on a self-harming state of mind that most people will never experience. Just as they are absorbing and processing this horrible new reality, and the shocking fact that I not only am saying it out loud but joking about it, I share the even MORE shocking fact that the folks in charge of her at that time allowed her to re-harm herself by continuing to provide her with sharp writing instruments in order to journal about her feelings.

The emotional journey of the joke includes both the shock of the reality of self-harm and the even more shocking failure of the "professionals." If this joke doesn't shock you, because your journey has included awareness of or experience with similar levels of self harm, then for you the joke is about the thrill of hearing such a taboo topic spoken out loud along with the validation of the very real failings of the mental health system.

There ought to be a frequent flier club at the ER.
You'd get to go through security, no waiting.
"Oh, hello, Mrs. Rolstad, you've been here twice this month! Here's your new PEOPLE magazine, you just head straight through those doors for preferential check-in and seating, AND you get a gift card for the vending machines!
We'll take your kiddo right back to her private suite and get her new beltless robe and slippers!"

Finding out we belonged under the NAMI umbrella

Comedy has also been the catalyst that helped me realize that my family and I belonged under the NAMI umbrella. Until I got involved with SMH, I had not considered them a resource for us, as in my mind our situation was not relevant to NAMI. In my mind, NAMI was only for people who were born with their mental illness, born with the genetic tendency to develop it. Our girls didn't have "that kind" of mental illness. We had no reason to expect the girls would have experienced any mental illness had it not been for their neglectful, abusive childhoods.

You see, it was clear their mental illness had been done to them, so it wasn't "real" mental illness. Was this denial or was it just flawed logic that had flourished because I'd not previously closely examined it? Either way, my time around NAMI folks made a few things abundantly clear.

Mental illness is mental illness, and it doesn't matter how a person gets there. Once you are there, PTSD, depression or anxiety are all equally real, equally debilitating, and equally draining on family members.

My only previous experience with NAMI was during my brief tenure with a different nonprofit which equipped and supported families of children with mental illness. It was in my time there working as a family advocate that I realized our girls, for all they had lost, were VERY blessed to be eligible for state-run and funded mental health care. I learned that often parents with private insurance find it extremely difficult to access adequate mental health care, or access enough of it, to help their child.

Finding out about the work NAMI does on a state and national level–encouraging science-driven research and lobbying for better access to health care and treatment–has been very encouraging. Hopefully, improvement in mental health parity and the Affordable Health Care Act will improve things for all families struggling with mental illness.

Yep, I'm a comedian

After a career of Earnest Do-Goodering in nonprofit management, and at least imagining myself on such a noble track for so long, it took a while to get comfortable with the idea that making people laugh was a worthwhile pursuit, and to feel confident saying

"I'm a comedian, writer and speaker." *(Believe me, I still giggle inside when I say it out loud.)*

The biggest adjustment was saying comfortably "I am an artist." Before comedy that would have been a ludicrous claim. My singing can make small children cry, my drawing abilities top out at vaguely representative stick figures, and no one really wants to see a chubby middle-aged mama doing hip-hop, no matter what wicked street moves I pick up in Zumba class.

Comedy, art? You know what? I would rather see a great comedian's act over and over again than listen to a symphony performance twice or revisit a painting in a museum. Each speaks to the human condition, each expresses experience and emotion. I am coming to terms with my artistic ability to sculpt words into sentences and sentences into experiences, and to infuse these "word-experience sculptures" with my own originality and humor. I am also coming to terms with how pretentious that sentence is.

I'm not gonna lie, having family members come up to me in tears after a show was initially disconcerting. Not the effect for which a comedian usually strives, you know? I often hear "How did you know? How did you know that's what we've walked through?"

If my comedy either opens the eyes of the regular person to the often absurd pain and difficulty of being a family member of someone who lives with mental illness, or validates a family member's experiences? Well, that's a worthwhile pursuit, tears, or laughter.

Signs that the friends you are visiting may be living with a teenager with mental illness

✓ There are alarms on all the doors and windows—on the INSIDE.

✓ There is nothing available to cut your steak but a butter knife.

✓ If you ask your host for a couple of ibuprofen, they have to unlock the medicine cabinet to get them for you.

✓ While the cabinet is unlocked, they can retrieve a steak knife for you.

✓ Refrigerator magnets all seem to be crisis lines, hospital numbers and emergency agencies instead of pizza joints.

✓ Their teen has a generous supply of soft clothes without drawstrings from recent vaguely described hospitalizations, often accessorized with socks with non-skid rubber patterns on the bottoms.

✓ News that the teen has been admitted to the hospital is shared with great joy, relief, and excitement! Yay!

✓ Instead of student council, sports or chess club, their teen's extracurricular activities include therapy, group therapy, skills training and DBT training.

✓ The teen is also surprisingly good at arts and crafts.

Hope for recovery

I realize as I write this that unconsciously, there are times when I still do not plan for or expect a full recovery for our girls. Currently, they are all living independently and are relatively stable. But on paper, it seems likely they may struggle their entire lives.

Any hope I do have for their recovery comes not from any therapist or physician, but entirely from the interactions I've had with other Stand Up for Mental Health comics. Each of these amazing adults is living and functioning to varying degrees while dealing with their mental health, and they have inspired me and given me hope for the girls.

Listening to my fellow comics, watching them take their difficult life experiences, shape those moments into comedy and share them with an audience, has been amazing and hope-giving. It is hard to put the weight and import of that hope into words, but to see others living meaningful, joyful lives despite mental illness has given me a critically important new lens through which to imagine our girls' futures.

That hope has made me fight even harder for them, it has made me push them harder and expect more from them, and it has helped me hold them accountable for achieving more of their innate potential. Conversely, it has also helped me step back as they approach adulthood and respect their right and ability to determine their futures.

Futures which I pray will be healthy, bright, and full of joy.

CHAPTER 5

ERIC

The other day someone asked me what it's like to have schizophrenia.
Well ... It's a little like questioning your sanity ...
and having your sanity answer you back!
—Eric

Eric's first performance was at a show in Tacoma, Washington. He was surprisingly quite nervous, even though he'd had plenty of previous speaking and performing experience. He was so nervous he had someone drive him up from his home in Vancouver, WA.

His material and his act were a work in progress. He knew that. He had rehearsed and rehearsed and although he was terribly nervous, he knew he would be able to perform. He started slow. Then the audience warmed up to him and people laughed. He made it through all his jokes and savored the applause that followed.

After the set, he went backstage and cried. It was such a relief to have done it, but in addition to relief, there was pride and a new sense of power over his situation.

I do take medications for hearing voices ... Thank you! Thank you! And there are a few ways to tell when my medications are a little off ... The best way to tell is when I... (Dramatically flair arms, turning ... pause for effect ...

Hold arms out like the cross ...) look up and say YES, GOD? Please don't be jealous just because my voices only speak to me! I know the voices are not real! It's just sometimes they have such great ideas! I would like to think I am up here representing the voiceless masses; unfortunately, those voices are all in my head!!

Although Eric has performed with us several times now, when we first met him all we knew was he was trained in Tacoma by David Granirer and had done a couple of shows up there. We needed one more comic for a Clackamas County show, so we asked him to perform with us at our first big show at Marylhurst University near Portland.

We saw his nervousness as he paced back and forth beforehand. During rehearsal, his voice cracked a couple of times. But when it was time to perform, he got stronger and stronger and about halfway through, when he could tell the audience was with him, he got a twinkle in his eyes.

This twinkle, this spark of confidence, we've each experienced it. It feels like adrenaline, with a calm and warming head rush. Your body warms and your voice becomes strong, and the delivery of each joke is better than the one before. Being onstage doing his routine felt awkward at first, but once he got used to it, it was nice to make people laugh. "It's empowering. Good for my self-esteem, and good for me to be able to share my story in a way in which I don't have to be ashamed."

Eric's set covers dark times, his schizophrenia, his voices, his counselors, and also his early life growing up gay in a big Christian family in Oklahoma. He deftly brings his audience along on his journey, all while putting a normal, goofy face on a scary label. When he is done, the audience is laughing and schizophrenia is not so scary after all.

To tell you a little about myself, I am from the beautiful mid-American town of Oklahoma City, where we are known for our dramatic acts of domestic terrorism ...

Or as I like to call it "Christmas with family" ... or "my love life" ...

After this act of domestic terrorism, I suffered a traumatic brain injury, and I lost my memory for a few months. I really thought I had died and gone to heaven. When I woke up in the hospital, I thought to myself "Hmmmmm. The food is good, everyone is in white, everyone is nice ... " and then the angel in white wheeled my bed over to the window. I looked, and frankly I was a bit disappointed.

I must have missed the rapture and I was one of the left behind! Instead of wings and a halo, I was in restraints and a neck brace. And heaven? Well ... heaven still looked like

Oklahoma to me!

I've had some really scary experiences. While I was hospitalized in one busy psych ward, a nurse said "Eric,

your behavior is strange and your eyes are fully dilated. So, we did some tests to find out if you are on street drugs."

After a bit she came back and proclaimed "I have some good news and I have some bad news! The good news is

you are not on street drugs. The bad news is (raspy voice) you're possessed by the devil!"

Actually, I was just angry. The psych ward was so busy they forced me to change my psychosis to Napoleon

Bonaparte, because Homeless Hippie Jesus was taken. And possession ... Well, that's still not covered by Medicaid!

Eric grew up in a church-going Oklahoma family, one of seven kids. His mom worked for the Federal Aviation Administration and his dad was an engineer for a local utility company. Eric had a great childhood and great parents who stepped in right away to get him help for his first hospitalization.

He was 19 when he had his first psychotic break. He'd been working and going to school and going to bars on the weekend. In hindsight, now he believes he was just self-medicating a growing mental health problem, a common coping mechanism for people with untreated mental health problems. Looking back now, he sees other signs of his impending mental illness as far back as his childhood. He would often be intensely sad as a child, but he was also highly creative and very smart.

At the time of his first breakdown, he wasn't making sense.

He slept on the couch all day and stayed up all night. He was saying weird things and hallucinated about being telepathic and hearing from God, or having telepathic communication with an alien being. With the hallucinations and the telepathy, he thought he was just a much more evolved human being. Remembering it now, it seems quite strange to him, but at the time it made total sense.

I think it is great that we can learn to laugh about a serious subject, I love the healing power of laughter.

Laugh and the world laughs with you, but laugh hysterically to yourself for no apparent reason and suddenly you're in a 72-hour hold!

Finally, one day his parents took him aside and said "Eric, you need to go to the hospital." He was hospitalized for 38 days. He doesn't remember all of it. He was diagnosed as depressed with psychotic tendencies, but he recovered quickly from that first break, and he was still functioning well.

Eric came out to his parents that he was gay when he was in his late teens, and it initially caused some family tension and separation, and he moved out. But his family fairly quickly came around to accept him. His sexuality hasn't caused him nearly the angst his mental illness has.

After high school he worked as a waiter, then started his own limo business that grew into an event-planning and decorating company. That went well for eight years until the Oklahoma City bombing, which was followed shortly by the World Trade Center bombings. Oklahoma air traffic and events around the airport plummeted, and he lost his business.

After another major breakdown, he wasn't hospitalized but instead, he took to the road with a truck-driver friend and traveled the country. Eric found the nomadic life was actually good for him. There was a routine schedule – up and on the road every morning, regular meals and regular sleep, and low stress. Slowly, he came back to himself.

In describing his disease when things are bad, Eric says it feels like his brain is eating itself from hyperactivity, and it's not good for his social life. "If you go to bars and talk to yourself or pace or tic, it just doesn't go over well." He is well aware that his diagnosis is one which can come with particularly socially unacceptable behaviors, and a particular stigma.

Eric moved to the state of Washington ten years ago, and that was the first time he received significant and meaningful mental health treatment. He now lives in Vancouver, WA with two friends and they have settled into a good life.

Eric's most serious breakdown came after learning he was HIV-positive. The stress of the serious diagnosis caused him to have severe hallucinations and paranoid thoughts, and he was hospitalized for several weeks. Hospitalization was followed by weeks of treatment at a day-treatment facility.

As he began to recover, he started volunteering at the facility and has since held several volunteer positions, each of which assisted in his recovery. He has served on boards for different organizations, including a regional Mental Health Advisory Board helping make policy recommendations and advocating for others with mental illness. Eric has also been to several mental health trainings and has plenty of certificates to prove it. He was out about his mental illness but very aware of the stigma, and selective with whom he would share his personal story for justifiable fear of rejection, or worse.

Before he did comedy, Eric facilitated a support group at NAMI. Several years ago, he began working part-time for NAMI in Clark County, Washington, leading weekly support groups. As a group facilitator, he provided a safe place for others to share and grow in their recovery, and he enjoyed the group as a place to share.

Another NAMI person told him about the SMH program, and he was intrigued by the thought of an opportunity to tell his story in an entertaining way. He saw comedy as a new challenge. He had seen a comedian perform one time, and in the back of his mind it had always been something he wanted to do. He thought it would be a great way to educate; Eric would be an advocate for anti-stigmatism and anti-discrimination and do something he thought would be fun. "I would be killing three birds with one stone." He applied for a scholarship to the class and got it.

He joined the group in the Tacoma, WA area for ten weeks, driving the 200-mile round-trip to Tacoma for classes as often as he could and participating by Skype when he couldn't. He didn't know what to expect but found that SMH founder David Granirer made him feel comfortable, as did his fellow students. "Everyone else was funny. And weird. Weird like me."

Through ten weeks of baring his soul and defining his story through humor, Eric rediscovered a part of himself that had lain dormant for decades. The impact was amazing. This Eric was outgoing, funny, relaxed, and open.

Some of his jokes are more than just funny. They are clever and deep.

I have a difficult time living with a mental health diagnosis and finding medical insurance. In desperation I had to find other alternatives to treatment such as pretending to be alcoholic to get free group therapy at the local 12-step meeting. However, getting Tasered by the police is still not a widely accepted form of electroshock therapy ... and it is definitely not covered by Medicaid!

For the first time in my working life, I had to apply for services to qualify for insurance. My therapist and I had to come up with a strategy because I had to interview with social security to get my determination for Medicaid. I didn't bathe for a week, I put gel in my hair for a messed up "do," I was nervous, and I had taken a triple dose of Seroquel. The case worker wrote "he looks like a smelly Ernestine with a drooling speech impediment." So remember, first impressions count! Don't be afraid to crazy yourself up for those important first meetings, first dates, or mug shots ... take Gary Busey!

By a round of applause, who here loves Facebook? or Skype? Yes ... yes. I see a few...

I tell you the 21st century is great for a germ-o-phobe like me ... I can now date online without actually having to touch anyone!! No, really, I'm just lazy ...

Facebook is getting way too big! The other day I got a message from God... it was an event invitation and apparently ... We have 3 mutual friends!

His stand-up experience has helped Eric in social situations, giving him more confidence to talk to new people and feel more at ease in conversations, and he's learned to tell a personal joke to break the ice. As Eric performs more, his newfound confidence continues to carry over into his personal life, and it has helped with his social awkwardness.

He appreciates that comedy has given him the opportunity to travel regionally for shows. "I'm able to perform which is great for my self-esteem. I'm on YouTube and Facebook which I have been able to share with friends, family and strangers."

He finds it a positive way to share, and to be, who he is. "I can look now at my inappropriateness and tendency to go too far when I'm talking as a gift, and not as a curse that should embarrass me. If I use humor to make people laugh, we can bond over that shared moment."

He finds that telling his story in a comedy routine is also a nice way to say, "I have schizophrenia, and I'm not just sucking the government dry as a recipient of social security disability payments."

I come from a good suburban Baptist family, with great parents, a brother, and sisters. We did however have our own special brand of dysfunction. I remember as a child, sneaking into my parent's bedroom, walking timidly up to the nightstand, and there I found a book that read "How to

Raise the Perfect Child Through Guilt and Manipulation."
It's a real book! Google it!

I like to call it the three R's of Dysfunction: Repression,
Regret, and Relatives ...

He even practiced his routine with his family, which was interesting because so much of it is about his family. "Mom liked those jokes," he says, "because she did use guilt and manipulation."

Before comedy he thought, "Why would you go to something like a class reunion?" He could hear the people now. "So, what do you do?" "Well, I take meds every day. Sometimes I get the runs. I try to avoid social security audits." There just was not a success story for Eric.

Now, comedy is something at which Eric is successful, and it has opened important new conversations with his extended family. After doing his routine for his family, a nephew came up to him and said, "We have something in common. I have schizophrenia too." They compared meds and it was a bonding moment that has stuck with his nephew.

I tell ya, insanity does not run in my family. It strolls
through, collecting billable hours ...

My family is very temperamental ... Half temper, and
half mental.
They don't suffer from mental illness, they enjoy it!

Helping others is a key part of Eric's recovery, and he regularly volunteers for Martha's Pantry, an HIV outreach ministry of Gentle Shepherd Church, Eric's own home of worship. He is particularly grateful that he has a church home and that he's found peace in his spiritual life.

When symptomatic, Eric's psychosis tended toward religious mania, and his breakdowns have frequently featured negative religious themes of judgment and shame. Thankfully now, he says, "I no longer feel God has turned his back on me. I love that I still thirst for God, and for worship. It means there's still hope for me."

Eric wants others to know that mental illness doesn't have to be a death sentence. He has to take care of himself, and he finds he is still triggered by loss and big family events, but his disorder is generally under control. He's currently on mild antidepressants, sleeping meds and his HIV meds. He hasn't felt the need for some time for the antipsychotics he uses to treat his schizophrenia when it's bad.

"I'm resilient, and when I do get sick, I get better pretty fast." His schizophrenia doesn't dictate his life or even his thoughts. At this point in his life, "when I go out to a bar to have fun and relax, I forget I even have a mental illness. I do all right for where I am, but it's not easy. It took me a while to get here, but now I'm in stable housing, in a long-term relationship, and I have people in my life who love me, care for me and check up on me."

"Really, I'm just a decent, hard-working, funny guy who tends to self-medicate and to be wildly inappropriate."

"All in all," he smiles, "I tolerate schizophrenia fairly well."

It is nice to finally be out about mental illness, but it is a bad sign when everyone in OUR Pride parade wears a bag on their head. Instead of Mardi Gras beads, they throw antidepressants. And the marching band uniforms are so hard to get into, because they lace up the back!!

Folks, no one is as dysfunctional as I am! Put it this way ...

I put the schizoid in schizophrenic ... I put the funk in dysfunctional ... I put the ass in Asperger's!

CHAPTER 6

MOLLY

My name is Molly, MD.
Little did I know going through med school the MD would
actually stand for Manic-Depressive. —Molly

Who are you if you've spent your whole life planning to do and be one thing, and then mental illness takes that away from you?

Who are you then?

That's the question Molly is trying to answer for herself. Molly is a young woman whose entire life trajectory has been diverted by severe mental illness.

Molly once had life all mapped out, her lifelong dream to become a family physician and return to serve her small hometown east of Vancouver, Washington. Today she is starting over, working on recovery from bipolar disorder and reformulating who she will be and how she will meaningfully contribute to her community now that mental illness has derailed her dream. Through comedy, she's found confidence, strength, and a new perspective to light her way forward to a new life and a new dream.

Ask Molly if she's always been funny and she admits with uncharacteristic shyness, "Ummmmmm, yeah. I've had a funny side. I think it's come out in the last few years more. I've been more willing to share it. I'm the classic younger sister. The youngest sister is typically funnier than the oldest." *(There are probably plenty of older siblings who would quibble with that, Tara included, but don't judge Molly. That's just how younger sisters are.)*

Long before she knew she was funny, Molly knew she wanted to be a doctor. She's known since she was a 7-year-old little girl taking her mom's anatomy book to bed every night.

"I was *that* kid"

Molly grew up in White Salmon, Washington, a small town perched on the steep hills above the Columbia River. Her mom was an elementary school teacher, and her dad owned a restaurant until she was about seven, and then worked as a restaurant supplier and at a payroll company. Molly was a motivated student and over-achiever from an early age.

"I was this nerdy student. I was voted Most Responsible; I was on every sports team. I wasn't in the 'in' clique, but I feel like I was friends with everyone. I was captain of the Knowledge Bowl team; I was a band geek. I was so achievement-oriented, I got 120% in one of my classes." She jokes that she's still bitter she wasn't voted most likely to succeed. After all, she had a 4.0 GPA, was number one in her class, and gave the commencement address. "I was friends with all the teachers; I babysat for them all. I was that kid." *(Maybe that kid lost a few Most Likely to Succeed votes to the anti-teachers-pet crowd? Jealous haters.)*

That kid knew exactly where she was headed. "In the 7th grade I told everyone I was going to come back to my hometown and be their doctor."

After high school she set off confidently on that path, beginning with college at Oregon State University in Corvallis and majoring in zoology even though she dislikes animals.

Why zoology for the girl who wanted to be a family doctor? "I hate animals," she says, "but it was the program most closely related to humans, closest to premed." Perhaps realizing how not warm and fuzzy that sounds, Molly restates her feelings. "Well, I don't hate all animals. I like domestic animals, and I do like animals you can eat!" The only other premed option for study had been biology, but that was out. She didn't major in biology because she would have had to study botany, and "I hate plants more than I hate animals."

After college, Molly was admitted to medical school at Creighton University in Omaha, Nebraska. That was when the lingering depression she'd been experiencing became severe, though she would not tell her family the truth or the depths of it until her first psych hospitalization almost four years later.

"I thought I could handle it"

"I'd kind of been trying to pretend I was 'normal' for years. I was depressed at the end of the first year of college. I told my folks when I went on antidepressants, but my parents didn't know how severe it was. My roommate knew, because she would help take care of me, but I graduated. My parents didn't know I had a mental illness for most of the time I had it, until I had my first manic episode. I was extremely depressed for pretty much all of medical school, awful, awful depression. My parents were incredibly supportive, not telling wasn't about them. I was just very independent, and I wanted to handle it on my own. I've always been really private, and people didn't know how I was feeling. I was really good at hiding it."

Her first hospitalization, halfway through her fourth and final year of medical school, changed all of that. Beginning New Year's Eve of 2008, Molly experienced her first manic episode. She was headed into her final term when the mania started. By this time, Molly had learned enough about mental illness, and treated enough patients with mental illness, that she was familiar with the various signs and symptoms of different disorders. That didn't make it easy for her to diagnose herself, however, or even accept the diagnosis from other physicians. "Probably about five days in I said 'wow, if I was bipolar, I'd think I was manic right now'. I didn't catch on to the fact that could be really happening, I really could be manic. I couldn't see it because I was manic."

Molly's mania continued for about five more days, and then her first post-manic depression set in. Molly was severely suicidal and depressed, and she was hospitalized. As the experts began the process of diagnosing Molly, bipolar disorder quickly rose to the top of the list. "They kept asking me if I'd ever had any of the symptoms on the list, but as a fourth-year medical student, I knew where they were going, and I'd deny it." Molly wasn't ready to accept this more serious diagnosis.

Hospitalization forced Molly to begin telling others in her life, including her fellow med students and medical school officials, what was truly going on. She might not have told her parents even then, were it not for her doctor. "At first, my folks knew I was hospitalized, but for the first week I kept telling them I was just there because my antidepressant medications were messed up, and I couldn't sleep. My doctor asked me, 'well, what do your parents know?' I told him 'they know what they need to know.'"

Her doctor forced the issue into the open, knowing how much Molly would need her family's support. He asked Molly directly if her parents knew she was suicidal. "I said 'yeeeaah,' but he called me on it. He could tell they didn't know. He told me that they would have to fly out to the hospital for me to be released, so I could tell them why I was there, and he could watch me tell them why I was there."

Shock and awe

Molly's hospitalization, and the severity of her mental illness, came as a complete shock to her parents. "She'd told us earlier, while she was in college, that she'd been on antidepressants but that was it. We thought she was fine. She seemed fine when she came home on the weekends," says Molly's mom, Jamie. "She kept everything very under wraps, let's say, she had become very good at it." The hospitalization changed all of that.

"That was our first hint anything was really wrong, our first shock, shock and awe. She'd had a month off around Christmas, but then she had the crash, and was suicidal. We got a call from our family physician, who said she needed to talk to us. Molly had actually called our family doctor from the hospital, told her what was going on, and told the doctor she needed to come and tell us. My doctor came over to our house."

Molly—who, some 15 hospitalizations later, is a little fuzzy on the details—interjects, sounding impressed with herself. "Oh, I forgot that was how that went down."

Despite Molly's thoughtful arrangements to get the news to her parents, it was still hard to hear. It all seemed horribly unreal to Jamie and her husband. "My physician is sitting right in my own living room with me and tells me that my daughter doesn't want to live."

Molly's parents flew out the next day, and their first visit to the hospital psych unit was traumatic, as it is for most everyone. "My husband and I went, and it was like Pollyanna goes to the psych unit, it was so scary. I'd never seen anything like it. There were locked doors, buttons to push and you could only go this far and then another button to push, and then all the people that were either sitting there looking at you or sitting there talking to themselves. And then I saw Molly." At this point, Jamie's voice breaks, remembering. "When I saw the medicated Molly, she looked like she was going to die. She just wasn't there. She sat in a meeting, we had family therapy or something, but she wasn't there."

At that point, the doctors had diagnosed Molly with bipolar I, but she hadn't accepted it yet, she was still calling it depression. The doctors did tell her parents she had a very severe mental illness that went beyond depression. "It was shocking," Jamie remembers. "My husband and I were both just like, in shock. This couldn't be Molly. This couldn't be happening, I mean, she'd made it through medical school, and she only had a few more months to go. It was just … shocking and sad and heartbreaking for her to have to go through what she went through."

Accepting the diagnosis and the severity of Molly's illness, along with the reality this is likely to be a lifelong struggle, has been a roller coaster for Molly and her family. Treatment has also been confusing, with so many hospitalizations, and with different doctors who have prescribed different medications for the same diagnosis. Although it is quite normal for treatment of severe mental illness to be more of a winding road than a linear progression, more of an art than an exact science, the situation lends itself to the temptation of family members to reach desperately for other, more "fixable" answers to what their loved one is experiencing.

"At first, we did spend a lot of time thinking that there must be something else. We were in denial. We knew she was suffering, but it had to be something else. It's so hard to admit in your brain as a parent—and we both felt this way—there could be anything wrong with your baby. She had a good childhood and a nice family, you know? Even though there wasn't anything, no childhood trauma or abuse, we imagined something must have happened to her, some kind of abuse, or someone hurt her, and we did so much second-guessing."

Molly's disease is genetic, either inherited or result of spontaneous mutation. Possible family genetic involvement includes a great grandma, as it seems likely from family recollections this grandma may have been bipolar. Of course, back then she was never diagnosed, but family members would talk about symptoms and delusions that she had, and, as Molly says, "It was like 'Duh, of course she was bipolar.' She sounds like a really good candidate for having had it!"

Dream interrupted

Despite her first hospitalization, Molly managed to graduate from medical school, and even began her residency in Spokane, WA. She enjoyed being a doctor, but after only three months, mental illness interrupted Molly's plans once again. There was another hospitalization, and she lost her job and her place in the residency program.

Being a doctor and being a patient too is really hard:

I know when I know more about something than they do ... Which is always

I seem to think I can be a doctor to myself ... which is probably why I end up in the ER frequently

... and nurses on the psych unit always tend to think I'm delusional. For some reason they don't take me seriously when I say "no really, I AM a doctor!"

She stayed in Spokane, living on disability insurance for

two years. In her mind it was just another temporary interruption. She was walking, getting healthy, and getting ready to attempt to do her residency again, "like Rocky, but not boxing."

Then Molly's dad died suddenly of a heart attack. The tragedy brought some of the most difficult moments Molly and her mom have faced in their relationship. Molly was fresh out of the hospital at the time, but doing well. Molly's mom, in the initial grief and shock of her husband's death, was terrified that if she called Molly to tell her what had happened that the news might trigger Molly and might make her suicidal. Jamie couldn't bear the thought of losing Molly too, so she sent her sister to tell Molly in person.

It can be hard for a family member to know the best thing to do when difficult news must be shared with their loved one who lives with serious mental illness. When they have had real cause to fear for their loved ones' safety because of the mental illness, it can be that much harder, and protective instincts can easily take over.

Molly was left angry and hurt that she hadn't gotten a phone call, that instead she found out by coming home to find her aunt in her living room. The hurt deepened when Molly put out a vague request for prayers on Facebook late that night, and several people responded immediately and specifically with their sympathies for the loss of her dad, making it clear that many in town already knew. Molly was left feeling like she had been the last to know, a tough feeling that compounded her grief.

Despite the loss of her father, and the significant nature of her mental illness, Molly pushed forward. She successfully reapplied for residency programs, and started over in Yakima, Washington, managing to practice medicine again. But in the end, after about nine months in her second residency, living with bipolar disorder and practicing medicine proved to be an impossible prescription for Molly.

As Molly says, "No one wants a doctor who is admitted to the hospital more often than her patients."

It became clear that she would have to give up on her lifelong dream of being a doctor. It was a painfully hard reality.

After Yakima, Molly moved home to live with her mom in White Salmon. That began a year of tremendous instability and chaos, with multiple hospitalizations. Molly loves her hometown and loves how supportive they have been of her mom, especially in the wake of her father's death. But living with severe mental illness in a small town where everyone knows you comes with its own special set of challenges.

When I was 30, I lived with my mom for a year, it was a little confusing being in an adult-adult child relationship.

She kept asking me if I needed to go potty before I drove her to McDonalds so she could buy me a Happy Meal, and I could have 5 minutes in the Playland if I ate all my McNuggets. It is a little awkward being a 300-pound, 30year-old woman in the ball pit ... and it can be kinda tight crawling through those tubes.

That year Molly was a regular visitor to the local hospital, which just happened to be the hospital where she had once expected to spend her medical career. The hospital had no mental health beds or unit, so if Molly needed inpatient psychiatric treatment she would have to be transferred to a different hospital or facility. This would lead to some of her funnier worst moments. "I'd go in for evaluation, and local mental health would assess me and try to figure out where to take me for treatment. If it was going to be an involuntary commitment (I was usually voluntary-ish, it would only be kind of involuntary) they had to take me out in restraints to the ambulance. Invariably people I knew would see me and wave, 'Hi, Molly!' I was in handcuffs so I couldn't wave back … yeah, it was embarrassing."

The nurses who worked at the small hospital all knew Molly. "The last weekend I lived there, I'd gone into the hospital and they couldn't find a bed for me anywhere in the state, not even in the state hospital, thank goodness. They just kept me in the hospital ICU where they could keep a close eye on me, since it's just like a big fishbowl. I just sat there in the ICU, all snug in a secure (i.e., locked down) room, and I was there in the fishbowl for three days waiting for a bed to open up somewhere. People would walk by while visiting their friends or family, poke their head in, 'Hi, what's going on in there?' I looked pretty healthy for the ICU! It was awful, but funny."

But not that funny. She's definitely not returned to that hospital since.

I've been hospitalized more than 14 times. Apparently, my coping skills aren't working.
Maybe it's time to switch from wine to vodka?

Just as she hadn't told her folks when she was struggling in medical school, Molly was still finding it difficult to be transparent with her mom when things weren't going well, even though Molly and her mom are close. "I hadn't told them back then because I didn't want to worry them, and because I thought I had it handled. That's common for me, and in the year I lived with my mom, I would often think I had it handled until I didn't. Then I'd just tell my mom 'Well, I need to go to the hospital now, my bag's packed, can you drive me over?' And she'd be like, 'Wait, I thought everything was ok?' 'Yeah, I've been working on this for a while, I've been talking to the crisis line and they say that either you take me or they're sending the police.'"

"It's such a small town and information travels fast. You tell someone in the grocery store and suddenly a stranger at the post office is asking you how your meds are working."

My therapist says I need to go to a grief group. So I joined a group, so far I'm the only one in it, just lots of talking to myself ... Doesn't seem that much different than usual.

Molly's journey to recovery has included grief counseling to help her deal specifically with the loss of her childhood career dreams. For now, that's been easier to achieve with a little more distance between Molly and her hometown. The hometown she loved so much turned out not to be a good place to be jobless, rapidly cycling between mania and depression, and grieving both the loss of her career and her father.

From the hospital that June she discharged to a treatment center, then in August of 2013 to day treatment and a new apartment 30 miles away in Vancouver. Moving to Vancouver really marked the start of a new life for Molly, where she is focusing on what and who she is now. Her disease has been somewhat more stable since the move, with only two hospitalizations. "Now in Vancouver, I'm more anonymous; it's just easier."

I go to the doctor a lot, so I spend a lot of time in waiting rooms.

When there's a big wait, I play waiting room bingo:

Adult in pajamas, check!

That person telling everyone else why they are there ...

Check!

Somebody complaining of a stomachache while eating Cheetos, child or adult ... Check!

Someone carrying a "puke bucket" ... Check ... and move away!

Judgmental person who should just mind their own business and read the outdated People magazine ... free space, that'd be me. ... Aaand BINGO!

Recovery: a full-time job

At this point, Molly lives with a severe case of rapid cycling, treatment resistant, Bipolar I. Most people don't realize recovery from mental illness is often a full-time job. Molly usually sees her therapist twice a week, her psych nurse once a week, and her prescribing psychiatrist once a month—all in addition to whatever group therapy she may be in at the moment.

Not to mention managing appointments with her neurosurgeon.

In addition to living with bipolar disorder, Molly lives with a separate condition that causes an unrelenting severe headache, which, when she started comedy, she'd had for almost a year. The headache is related to a condition that is causing fluid buildup in her brain, unrelated to her bipolar disorder. She's had a couple of brain surgeries, first having a shunt implanted to remove the fluid and then, after she got an infection in the shunt, surgery to have it removed. Currently the headache is at a relatively constant "dull roar," and she is planning to get the shunt re-implanted as soon as her doctor tells her it's possible. "At that point, I had a lot of other things going on, and just about then I found out how serious my headache was. They told me 'You may have this headache for the rest of your life.'"

I've had a headache since September. The first brain surgery didn't work, maybe I should have started with Tylenol?

Yeah, I had another brain surgery a couple weeks ago, no big deal, it's not like its brain surg ... well, it's not rocket science.

Molly and her therapist are working hard on coming up with a safety plan for Molly's manic cycles, when Molly may put herself at high risk through poor decision-making. "What I need," Molly says, "is a safety plan I'll follow through on when I'm manic. 'Cause when you're manic you don't give a damn! I need a plan that intervenes when I'm the most dangerous to myself."

Finding that plan, and then sticking to it, is made particularly hard by the nature of mania: it feels great, at the beginning, and it can be difficult for Molly to recognize that it is even happening. "Usually, the mania is fun the first few days. I'm shopping with whatever money I have (which would be about ten bucks most of the time) or eating out more, shopping at a fancier grocery store, getting more creative. It starts with that, that's the first few days. Then I'm like, hey … it would be fun to have some fun with someone else. My mania often includes hypersexuality, which is really NOT my game in real life. That part of my mania can get me into dangerous, intense situations, and usually lasts for a couple of weeks."

If there is an upside, it is that the extravagant and irrational decisions that Molly has made while manic have provided great fodder for her comedy routine. "If my dad was still alive," Molly says, "he'd tell you all the crazy details, like when I called him for more money because I'd spent all my money at Costco on a manic Costco fruit-buying binge. When I'm manic I don't really have thoughts, or a plan, just brilliant ideas. I just knew I needed fruit, so I just loaded my cart up with all of those giant plastic fruit containers. Of course, it was January, so it was extra expensive Costco fruit! I ate smoothies for weeks." She's also bought hundreds of dollars of cake decorating supplies, started a Mary Kay business even though she never wears makeup, and flown first-class to Las Vegas, placing personal ads for dates.

As I mentioned, I have bipolar disorder. Things get pretty "interesting" when I'm manic.
One manic episode, I started a Mary Kay business.
I don't wear make-up.
I am a terrible salesperson.
… Still no pink Cadillac, but I do have a basement full of lipstick and anti-aging cream.
Makeovers at my house after the show?

Another time when I was manic I went to a craft store and bought every single cake decorating supply they had. I think my cat's tired of having birthdays now, but she seems to like the birthday parties better than she liked the Mary Kay makeovers …

My mania takes me places. One time it took me all the way to Las Vegas … First Class.

Some people go to Vegas to get married. I didn't get married, but I consummated a few!

Although sometimes funny in retrospect, Molly acknowledges the way she acts when she is manic often increases her shame and isolation later. "I learned I can't be open with my friends about this; it's too hard for them to understand. I've definitely alienated a few of them."

Molly may put herself in danger from others when she is manic, but it's what happens after the mania when she is most at risk to herself. "When I need to be hospitalized, it is usually because I am severely depressed, usually after a manic episode."

"Post-manic depression feels different than regular old, run-of-the-mill depression. There is a desperation, because it just keeps happening. My desperation to end the depression becomes nearly indescribable, I'll try anything to make it stop, which is when I wind up in the hospital. They always know they have to put me in the room with the cameras and check my pockets at that point, I'm so desperate."

You meet a lot of really disturbed people at psych hospitals, and the patients are in tough shape too.

I met a guy in the hospital last year. We had so much in common: we spent our days coloring, we liked long walks in a locked hallway, and we both liked to be tied up!

Acceptance

Without question, the most intense stigma Molly has faced since her diagnosis has come from inside herself. Molly thinks this self-imposed stigma resulted from her exposure to the most severe cases of mental illness in her medical school training hospital. "I saw the worst bipolar cases, and the worst of this or the worst of that in medical school. I learned what can happen, and I internalized that. I thought 'oh, if I have bipolar disorder that will be me.' It kind of got worse as my symptoms got harder and harder to control. It was like well, I know where this is going, I've treated it in the hospital. I'm going to be that 60-year-old lady who melts down and is washed up."

Her biggest fear had definitely been what people back home would think, and until recently she believed most people in her hometown had no idea why Molly was back from medical school but not working as a doctor. How was she going to tell all her friends, family, and acquaintances?

The short answer was that at first, she wouldn't. After she quit medicine and returned home when she saw friends and acquaintances at social functions or on the street, some would ask, "When are you coming back to open your practice, to be our doctor?" She would dodge the question, because she was afraid to tell them the truth, afraid they wouldn't understand or still accept her.

Molly was surprised to learn recently from her mom that most people in town already knew about Molly's struggle with mental illness, as Jamie had been open with people almost from the beginning. "Oh, yeah, the community knew. At first, I didn't know what to say, but I would say she's been diagnosed with bipolar, it's a rough road and you have to get treatment and figure out how to get the help you need. I kept it kind of simple. But I haven't kept it from anybody, I think they need to know. I'll just lay it out. I'm not embarrassed, I feel like I'm an educator." Molly's even been on the prayer chain at the local Methodist church, which was news to Molly. "Really?"

she asks. "I guess I've made the big time!"

Neither Molly or her mom have ever gotten any negative or unhelpful responses from anyone in White Salmon, and the community has been supportive. So why didn't they say anything, why didn't Molly know that they knew? Perhaps it was partly due to the hidden nature of mental illness. If Molly had looked like she'd broken her leg—cast, crutches, etc.— but they weren't sure, they probably would have just asked. But because mental illness is mostly invisible, people don't feel comfortable asking. "Although," she says, "I'm sure that any of them in the vicinity of the emergency room or the hospital a few times, I'm sure they figured it out."

As Molly has come to accept her disorder, and accept the necessity for safety and treatment plans, she's been able to give herself the grace to forgive herself and to be realistic about life with bipolar disorder. "I can't just stop what I'm doing or how I'm feeling—feeling sad, the cycles, or the behaviors. It's impossible. I accept that I'm gonna make stupid decisions. I'm gonna try not to, but I'm gonna wind up in the hospital. I'm hoping I can stretch it out further, but I can't see it as a failure if I wind up there. It's used as a tool for my treatment, not a punishment."

"I remember," says Molly, "the first time I had someone tell me 'you're going to have to deal with bipolar disorder for your whole life, it may get a little better, it may get a little worse.' I was like, 'no it's not.' It's true, it's a lifelong struggle, a chronic illness, it took me a while to come to that but it's true. Early on, I thought I was just depressed, I was gonna come out of it. Now I know that it's a chronic illness."

Losing weight is hard. I lost almost 100 pounds a couple years ago, only to gain it back due to medications ... and French fries.

People keep telling me to exercise, and I am. I'm exercising my right to eat ice cream!

"I gotta contact these people"

Molly knew she needed to be a part of Stand Up for Mental Health as soon as she saw the comics in action. She had gone out with a friend to a local Vancouver, WA, NAMI event, a holiday dinner for consumers of mental health services in the area. She had not had big hopes for the night and arriving at the event didn't help. She and her friend had gotten dressed up since it was a holiday dinner, but arriving at the dinner it became clear that many of the others either hadn't gotten the holiday dress code memo, couldn't dress up or were in no mood to do it.

"I felt so out of place, 'cause a lot of the other clients, they seemed like they were from different backgrounds, or maybe more disabled than I was. They hadn't dressed up, and they weren't laughing. I felt like my friend and I were the only ones laughing at the jokes! I was down in the front row, and I thought, "Oh, my God, these people are awesome, I have to call and join them. I thought they were hilarious, even when Santa interrupted Tara, and I wanted to be a part of it." *(Authors' note: yes, Tara was actually interrupted mid-routine by Santa, whose timing, frankly, stinks. But when it comes to comedy and performing priorities, Santa wins, hands down. Put your jokes down, and back away from the jolly man in red.)*

At the time of the dinner, Molly was significantly depressed. "I had just come out of a pretty big manic episode and I was on the big downside. I'd just finished a day treatment program, I'd only been out of that for a few days. Going to that event really felt like an acknowledgment of 'Wow, is this what my life has come to?' I mean, there were adults in pajamas there, it was rough, it was depressing. 'Adults in pajamas at holiday dinner, check!'"

In the midst of being depressed at what was—for her—a depressing event, seeing the SMH comics was just what Molly needed. "It gave me hope; I was like 'I gotta contact these people, I could do stand up.' I was so excited, because ever since I got sick, everyone had been telling me 'Oh, this is going to be so great for your stand-up routine someday,' but I'd never think I'd actually do it."

She looked up the Clackamas County SMH troupe online and immediately registered for the next class, which started in February of 2014. From day one, Molly carried herself with the air of someone who has a history of being successful, who is used to being good at what she does, and who has been told she was funny. In fact, she is naturally funny, quick on her feet and bubbly.

When Dave and Tara first met Molly, it was the first day of that spring's comedy class. The first thing they noticed was Molly's smile. The students went around the table introducing themselves and when it was Molly's turn, she spoke a bit haltingly at first, although clearly. Honest and open about her mental illness, she shared her experiences as a doctor and her struggles and challenges with her illness. And some of the stuff she said, she said in a funny way. As he listened it was clear to Dave that she got it. He thought "Boy, she is really going to fit in." He didn't know yet how right he was.

Molly in comedy class wasn't the Molly she had historically been. It was a surprise to the class that Molly thought she needed to work on assertiveness, but before comedy she'd been quiet, shy, and passive. It was almost like she had made the decision to come into comedy class as the Molly she was working to become. Today she is still working to integrate the Molly-people-can-walk-all-over with sassy-confident-Comedy Molly.

But even Molly-in-process was a breath of fresh air. As she shared, she made it safe for others to talk about their experiences. After a while, others began to defer to her as the resident comic among the student comics.

"I was excited in the first class, 'cause there were a lot of people, but I could tell that I was one of the people that was there to do it, you know. I'm competitive, and I could tell I was one of the funny ones," she says. "I would write a lot of jokes after each class."

Boy, would she! Molly's prolific joke writing shined from her first homework assignment, which was to come back the next week with two punch lines, two set ups or two complete jokes. The morning after the first class, Dave got an email from Molly with four jokes that she had written the previous night right after class. Sure, the jokes were a bit rough and needed editing. But it was clear Molly had some serious funny inside her.

The next day she sent two more jokes, and then two more and two more. Molly's jokes usually begin with a true premise and many with a true punchline. Sometimes she takes creative license and creates a funny punchline. Most of her jokes are based in reality, and by the time she's perfected them, they are meaningful, poignant, and funny.

To begin with, of course, some were funny, some were not. Dave would tell her which were funny and why, and which were not funny and why. She digested the recommendations and would rewrite the not-so-funny ones and continue to edit the funny ones to make them better, refining them in class with Dave and Tara. She was putting in more time than anyone else and the results showed it.

Molly says that getting involved with SMH helped smooth her next bipolar cycle, partly triggered by the bad medical news about her potentially lifelong headache. "I didn't get manic-y. I did have one mental health hospitalization that March related to stress over my headache. But it was a shorter hospitalization than I'd ever had. After that, I went the longest stretch I've gone without a psych hospitalization. Comedy has been a good coping skill, and I credit comedy for keeping me out of the hospital. I've had a couple of mania's here and there, but they haven't been as big.

I've got a lot of doctors: a psychiatrist, a family doctor, a neurologist, a neurosurgeon, an ear, nose, and throat doctor, a neuro-ophthalmologist, and a gynecologist.

I'm always going to appointments.

You'd think by now they'd have figured out that I'm really just lonely ...

I also see a therapist. My therapist and I have been working on assertiveness for months. Hopefully, in a few more months, I'll be able to assertively ask for a new therapist.

My therapist has been trying to teach me about boundaries, like the restraining order she got against me.

Her coming-out show

By the time it was time for her class to do final edits and put their final sets of about 15 jokes together, Molly had over 40 jokes to choose from. Molly and Dave started her editing process, and the rest of the class jumped right in with ideas, suggestions, and favorites.

They initially got the set down to 30. Then 25 and then 20. The last 20 were all so funny, it would have been a shame to cut any out. Dave decided to extend Molly's set and have her tell all 20 jokes. Her set would be closer to ten minutes than the five-minute sets he normally shoots for, but he knew it would be ten minutes of good material.

Molly's delivery was great. The way she told her jokes was very funny. In rehearsal she worked on slowing down her pace. It's natural to be nervous and go too fast. We worked on pausing at the end of each joke, so people had time to get it and to laugh. After a couple weeks of practice, she had it down, and the only thing to do was get up there and perform, go on stage and share her story, one joke at a time.

As the date of the show approached, she invited several people to come, both new and old friends. She told people in White Salmon about it. She put it on her Facebook page. She was doing stand-up comedy, she was coming out about her mental illness, and she wanted everyone to know. She was ready.

Ready, yes, and also still a bit apprehensive because she didn't know how people would react. Was she sharing too much? Was it too real? Would people get her jokes? Would people laugh? But Molly was determined to do it.

The night of the show, Molly arrived early, and was excited, even giddy. Dave constructs the shows with strong opening and closing sets, and he knew Molly would be the perfect finale for this show.

She got more excited as the evening went on, especially when she saw how receptive the audience was for the comics. Most of our fellow comics arrive at their first show nervous and either alone or with 1-2 close friends or family. Molly had a full posse in attendance, including her mom, an aunt, some friends from White Salmon, and family from nearby who all came to support her.

The first couple of jokes she ran through a bit too fast, but she realized it and slowed down. She gave the audience time to laugh, and in so doing she was able to enjoy the laughter. "I was like 'People are laughing, this is good, they're laughing. And at the right time.' I thought I was doing pretty good, and then I started the one about having had a headache since November, and everyone laughed." She laughed along with the audience at some of her jokes and that made them even funnier.

Molly was so self-confident right from the beginning of her first show, she found herself critiquing the audience's response while she was doing her act. "I thought, 'wait, that's not the funny part. That's not the punch line, that's the set-up, you're not supposed to laugh about that.' Then when I got to the punch line they didn't laugh as much as they had for the set-up! I was thinking 'they totally ruined my joke.'"

But Molly rolled with it and went on, her analytical mind tracking along with her joke mind, noting which jokes got applause, which ones seemed to be funnier. "Then I did my joke about liking to be tied up and I made the mistake of making eye contact with my mom, which was funny."

By the end she was smiling ear to ear. She did it. And she did it well. "When I was done, I remember I felt like, 'I think I did ok!' Then when I got down off the stage, one of the other comedians said, 'You killed it!' My friends and family were all really happy and proud of me, which was awesome. I was just on a high. There'd been so much buildup, and I didn't mess up."

The performance high continued, and Molly didn't sleep all night that night.

Unexpected reactions

That first comedy performance changed everything for Molly, who had been nervous about sharing the video online. Being more open with others about her bipolar disorder hasn't prompted the reaction Molly feared it would. Instead of negative reactions, fear or rejection, the majority of responses have been positive. "I'm friends with just about all of White Salmon on Facebook and I wanted to share it with them because I thought I did a pretty darned good job. I think it was pretty well received. I got some private messages that were like 'I didn't know,' or 'my sister has bipolar', and some public messages that were like 'Wow, Great!'"

"I guess I expected this big negative reaction like 'OMG, you're CRAZY,' or all this stuff I had in mind. I hadn't really played it out. I don't know what I was afraid of. I was afraid of rumors, I guess.

Now I'm hearing good rumors, about people saying, 'Have you heard her stand-up?' Facebook is kind of my little world; I don't have a lot of friends yet in Vancouver. Putting my little YouTube video up on Facebook was like my coming out party, and as I watch how many have viewed it, I think 'OK, now that many more people know'. Now I think it's great, and I tell people to watch it. You're going to learn more about me than you want to know, and it's mostly true. Most of my jokes are based in reality. No, I may not have any restraining orders against me, but I've been to Las Vegas, and, uh … enjoyed it. When I was living with my mom, I was in the hospital every couple months. I've been in the hospital 14 times in five years. That joke is really true. Seven of them were within a year. It was a rough go of it there for a while."

When people see my mom in White Salmon, now she gets a lot of questions about my comedy from people around town. They'll say 'Oh, I saw Molly on YouTube, she's great,' but they also say, 'Is Molly really sick?' My mom will say 'Yeah, she's been sick for years now, 5 years.' I don't know if I would have told everyone without the comedy, and I'm kind of proud of myself. I was really proud of myself, performing."

Coach bags and food stamps

Molly's comedy frequently focuses on opening audiences' eyes to the day-to-day indignities of life on disability. Those indignities came as quite a shock to Molly. Her family had always lived comfortably, and before her bipolar disorder Molly had been well on her way to a life of financial security in medicine. As a resident, she had already begun making a significant salary, and she still has several nicer things she had treated herself to, like expensive Coach purses and bags. Now, she's writing new jokes about being a doctor on welfare with an eye towards educating and entertaining.

"When you take your Coach purse to the grocery store and whip out your food stamp card, people give you dirty looks." It's a bit of a no-win situation for her, she says, only half-joking that she's not sure what she is supposed to do. "I bought it when I had a substantial income. What, am I supposed to sell my Coach bag and buy a cheap purse at Target to match my food stamp card, just to make people feel better?"

She has a smartphone, which also makes people's eyebrows raise judgmentally. Not so fast, she says. "Yes, I have an iPhone. My old employer bought it for me, it's three years old, and my mom pays the bill. But you can't tell people all of that in the grocery store line."

"Being on food stamps definitely means at the end of the

month, I probably have food, but it doesn't go together, and I'm eating weird things for breakfast." She has no idea where people get the idea that people on government benefits such as disability are "livin' large" on the government dime. "On disability, what I would have made in a day as a doctor, is now my income for a month. You try to make that work."

Speaking of medical school, I have a lot of debt, and living on social security, not a lot of ability to pay it off, so I get a lot of collection calls. They typically go like this: "Hi, is this Molly M?" Uh, I guess.

"Could you provide your date of birth for me for identity purposes?"

At this point I realize they are going to try to get money out of me, with little result.

"Dr. M, I'm calling because you have an outstanding student loan balance of $356,542 and I'm wondering how you'd like to take care of that today? Visa? Check by phone?"

Well, I have $12 left in the bank until next month, so, I could give you $2 of that, would that help?

"When do you think you'll have the money? Should I call back next month?"

I'm looking forward to our next chat.

It isn't just judgment or reactions from strangers that Molly has to navigate.

Money-related interactions with old friends, particularly friends from college and medical school, can get awkward and complicated. One of her closest friends is a successful veterinarian who owns her own clinic on the Oregon coast. When Molly visited for the weekend, her friend asked her to go to the grocery store and pick up ingredients for a salad for that night's dinner. "So, I did," says Molly, "and I paid for it with my food stamp card. When she told me she'd pay me back, I said ok, and I left the receipt on her counter."

When she saw the receipt, Molly's friend was an instant bundle of embarrassment, concern, and upper-class guilt, both worried about Molly and probably concerned about eating food-stamp-funded salad. "She came to me all upset, 'oh no, you paid for this with your food stamp card? I didn't want you to do that.' I was like, 'Well, why not? It's food, and I don't have any cash.' 'But' she said, 'why would you use your food stamp card? Aren't you going to be out of food stamps?' She just wasn't understanding that was my only option. That's how I buy food."

The same friend struggles to understand Molly's behaviors when she is manic or depressed. Before Molly, her friend had no reason to have a deep understanding of bipolar disease or mania. "Just because someone in your life loves you, doesn't mean they understand your mental illness. She'll say 'Well, why don't you just stop ... doing those things?'" It's not that simple.

Like any other single woman, I have a cat. And like any other cat, mine's only nice on her terms. She's also technically my therapy cat. Who knew that therapy involves being ignored, bitten, and scratched?

At least she doesn't charge a copay.

Something to be proud of again

When asked to characterize herself before and after the comedy class in a few words, she's quick to say "Before, I was on this hopeless track. Now I've got something in my life, some hope, something to look forward to."

"Not only that, but I made the traveling team!" she says. In fact, Molly has now become a regular performer with the SMH troupe, and after her second show, she told Dave it was a relief to be good at something again. "I used to think I was good at medicine, at being a doctor, I guess I can say that even though I lost my job, I was good at being a student doctor for sure. For the last couple of years, I haven't been good at doing anything, except maybe cooking dinner every now and then. Now I'm good at comedy, and it's nice to have something I'm good at, a skill. Nice to have something I'm proud of myself for, and at the end of the day I can look back on that and say, yeah, I'm a stand-up comedian."

This confidence and pride in her comedy has become a critical lifeline during the lows of her mood swings. "When I'm manic, I'm great, I'm sure I'm good at everything, I'm going to save the world. But now, when I'm depressed, I can play my video and remind myself that I'm good at this. Reminds me that I've got purpose, and that there's more to me than my headache, or being depressed, or doctors' appointments. When I was a doctor, I had something to be proud of. I have something to be proud of again."

Molly's comedy even serves as a coping mechanism for her mom when she is having her own rough days. "When I get really down, I watch her comedy video too. It's life, if you can't laugh about it, it's too hard to be in it."

You don't need coping skills until you need them

When life is grand, and proceeding as you had planned, you don't need good coping skills. The more easily success comes to you, the more surprised you may be when life goes south and you find yourself woefully unprepared. Molly—always good at school, always successful at what she tried—has certainly experienced that. "I didn't have good coping skills before comedy, and that's what I'd really been working on in therapy. Now, comedy is a good coping skill. Last time I was in the hospital for emergency brain surgery, I was writing jokes and texting them to Tara from the ER waiting room."

Comedy has given her the ability to approach difficult situations in an entirely new way. On one recent trip to the ER, Molly experienced something that happens far too frequently to people with mental illness — she went to the ER as a medical patient but got stereotyped and mistreated as a psych patient. Post brain surgery, she'd gone in to the hospital ER with a fever, as her neurosurgeon had instructed her that any fever needed to be evaluated at the ER in case of infection. But she made the "mistake" of telling them that because of the fever and pain she was having trouble sleeping, and that she was concerned the disrupted sleep schedule could trigger her mania. That changed things. They started to treat her as a psych patient. Instead of a thorough post-surgical check for infection, she went home with additional antipsychotics after a pat on the head and 45 minutes with the social worker. *(Authors' note: Yes, even in the medical field, discrimination against mental illness is alive and well.)*

She was angry. In the past, the dismissive mistreatment would have stuck with her for days and kept her awake at night. She would feel helpless because she had no control over the situation or her feelings. After ruminating about the incident, she would have stormed back to the hospital and told them off. Then afterward, because Molly is really a nice person, she'd have felt guilty and despondent.

But this time processing the events was different because of her comedy experience. "After I got home, I thought about how the whole situation was really funny. Before I would have been really angry, or called a crisis line about it, and it would have stayed with me for a while. Instead, I went home, wrote a joke about it and that was that." Instead of sticking with her and keeping her up, it was over. She slept well that night. It didn't control her life the way it would have before. She was discovering that comedy as a coping skill gave her control over the situation. "Now I've told the joke to several people and they think it's funny. It's given me a whole different way of dealing with these types of things."

Now when something inevitably triggers her, her reaction has changed. She sits down to write a joke about it. She finds the humor in it and the trigger passes. She escapes the old pattern of vaulting into mania or sliding into dark depression.

Mom's new role: family member of a loved one with mental illness

Now that people know Molly's story, Jamie finds that they open up to her about their experiences with mental illness.

"People say to me all the time now, 'Oh, my sister or my mom has bipolar or is depressed', mental illness is all around us."

Molly's mom is well aware of how much work it is just for Molly to manage her disease. "I admire her for sticking to being compliant, taking her medications, keeping herself healthy and safe. It's a hard job, and she's doing it and I'm so happy. I know there are so many that won't or can't take their medications."

All the admiration in the world, however, doesn't allay Jamie's maternal anxiety about Molly's well-being. Some of the anxiety is practical. "As a mom, it concerns me all of the side effects she is exposed to with the medications."

Some of the anxiety is much deeper. "There is a little bit of fear in me, ok, a lot of fear in me that something will happen to her. I don't want to lose her."

Jamie has never been with Molly when she is really manic. Molly confirms this is intentional, that she shields her mom from her when she is experiencing mania, and the accompanying unsafe, uncharacteristically hypersexual behavior. That hasn't shielded Jamie from a mother's fear. "I've never been with her, but I've heard it in her voice," Jamie says. "I can hear it and it makes me really scared, because when she gets manic, I know she does things that are really dangerous. I'm afraid someone is going to kill her, and I have no freaking control over that either. I don't sleep those nights until I hear her voice the next day. Of course, in some ways, the good news is that she doesn't have any money so she can't go shopping, although I think shopping takes the edge off. Sometimes I'm just tempted to give her a hundred bucks and say, 'go shopping, just don't touch anybody!'"

The really scary part for Jamie is knowing that in those times, Molly really doesn't have the ability to say for herself "That is dangerous."

"Especially when she had always been such a competent, 'I've got it handled,' successful student. Maybe," Jamie jokes with her daughter, "Maybe if you had been a rebellious brat in high school, it would have been easier. But instead, you were the kid who easily won my challenge of $1000 if you got through high school with no drugs and alcohol."

There have been other particularly tough times, Jamie remembers. One of the most difficult was taking Molly for ECT treatments. Jamie drove Molly to the last in a series of three "shock therapy" treatments that she was prescribed in Spokane, before the doctors decided the risks to Molly were larger than any benefit she was getting. (ECT treatment, while it can be dramatically effective in reducing symptoms such as depression for some people, can also result in short-term and permanent memory loss and cognitive problems.) Jamie recalls how frightening it was to wait for Molly during those treatments. "I would sit out there just sick, afraid they'd fry the wrong part of her brain, afraid she'd come out and not be able to have a conversation, but at the same time hoping against hope that the treatment would just re-set her brain, rejoggle it and she'd come back and just be 100%, fine, no more medication necessary."

Through Molly's diagnosis and illness, as well as the loss of her husband, Jamie has learned a lot about herself. "I've learned that life is uncertain, I'm stronger than I thought I was, and I can handle just about everything. I've learned that I have a really strong daughter, and I'm very happy about that. I've learned that other people all around me have similar stories, but you don't know that until you are in crisis and then they open up."

Grief is still very much a part of Jamie's days, grief over her husband and the retirement they'd hoped to spend together, and grief over Molly's illness and loss of the career her daughter had planned for herself from early childhood. "It's been so hard to see Molly lose her way and lose all her dreams she's had since she was that little girl asking me for my anatomy book. It was so great how she always knew what she wanted to do."

As time has made those wounds less raw, she has begun to more actively seek both healthy ways to combat her own feelings, like yoga classes and time with friends, and also ways to help others. Since retirement, Jamie has volunteered with a children's grief group, and she is thinking about starting a loss or grief group for adults in her area. Such a group is lacking in their small hometown, although Jamie is grateful for the services that Molly has found in Vancouver.

"Other family members should know that especially in bigger cities, there is a whole network of people out there to help your family member that you don't even know about. It's not easy living in a small town and being mentally ill."

Jamie is also still exploring ways in which Molly's illness has changed her own perceptions and perspectives. "We have one person in our little town who walks the streets talking to himself. I look at him differently now. And it changed me as a teacher, it actually made it harder for me to teach. When kids were in crisis, I felt them plugging into my heart so much deeper. I was so much more aware, and sensitive. They'd already called me the touchy-feely teacher." That new, rawer empathy made it too hard for her to teach, especially in an environment in which teachers were being pushed to teach to standardized tests. That dichotomy led, in part, to Jamie's recent retirement from teaching.

I was in the psych hospital recently.

I tell you what, when you get out, never forget your cell phone at home while you go out for a day of errands and a bite to eat, or your missed calls from your mom go something like this:

10:00 am: "Hi honey it's Mom, call me back when you get a chance!"

10:45 am: "Hey, you must be busy, please call me back."

12:00 pm: "OK, are you doing alright? Call soon!"

1:30 pm: "Something's wrong, isn't it?!"

1:45 pm: "Of course I trust you to take care of yourself, but are you taking care of yourself?"

2:00 pm: "OK, since you haven't called me back ... what do you need me to do?? What hospital are you at? What did you do already?"

2:05 pm: "OK, I've called the police and the state patrol. You're too old for an Amber Alert. Where are you???"

2:06 pm: "I've got your brother flying in from New York to be with me, please call if this is some sort of sick joke, it's not funny anymore!"

I didn't even know there was a problem until I arrived

home to the candlelight vigil on my front lawn.

"It's going to be really good, down the road"

When it comes to her mom's hopes and dreams for Molly, they're pretty basic. "I want her to be happy and productive, that's all, and that's what comedy has done for her. The happiest I've been in the last few years was seeing the spark of Molly come back with comedy. I haven't seen Molly this happy in a long time. She's always been funny, like her dad was. Her funniness is back, and her dad shines through every time she does a joke. Comedy has been a lifesaver for her, like a rope you threw to her. It made the rest of her life, whether grief counselor or job counselor, go better. She'd come out of those meetings more upbeat and positive, full of life, like there are options. She's come alive again."

Molly, at the age of 31, has just gone through a major career change, so her path is still unclear. She knows she can't go back to school, because of the small detail of $350,000 in outstanding medical school debt. No one will give her loans. She can't do anything too stressful, because it will trigger the bipolar. "That pretty much leaves yoga teacher," she says, "and I hate yoga!"

Molly does not see herself ever practicing medicine again. She would have to go through residency again, and as she's already tried twice, she says, "It would just be unheard of to get a third chance. If I'd almost made it, and gotten pneumonia or something, maybe, but having to leave twice for mental illness, no hospital wants to take that chance."

She's thinking she'll probably avoid the whole medical

field, really, as she doesn't think she'd be successful as any kind of paraprofessional. "I'd either be like 'Well, you're doing this wrong, I'm a doctor and I know,' or I'd be all 'I'm going to go hang out with the doctors now, cause I'm in that club.' And they'd be like 'No … you're the receptionist.'"

She's not sure about kids and marriage. She'd like to have both in her life but isn't sure how that's going to work with being on meds or having been involuntarily hospitalized.

It hasn't been easy for the former straight-A student to let go of the over-achieving identity she created through accomplishment after accomplishment. It's not clear now what her future holds, but Molly realizes she needs to find a new way to define who she is, and what a successful life will look like.

Molly's mom Jamie has an idea. "We don't know why Molly's path to being a doctor was interrupted and everything has taken a different turn, but I have to have hope that whatever she's going to go on to next will be really powerful or important. She can be a spokesperson in a way that is loving, compassionate and caring; she's been there, and she knows what it's like. She knows that living with mental illness wouldn't be anyone's first choice. I have a knowing in me that there is going to be a path for her that's really important, she wasn't put on this earth to just do nothing. She's an amazing woman. Whether it's to make people laugh, or make people cry, or help people she has a passion to help, she's an amazing person who will find that path."

Now, Molly's newfound comedy skills help her navigate the mania and the depressions of her bipolar disorder, and she believes comedy has helped her dramatically reduce her hospitalizations. That is a significant outcome by itself, but there's more.

Comedy has given Molly a new set of tools with which to forge her new identity, a new Molly. Comedy has also given her the venue through which to communicate her reality. In addition to a good laugh, she hopes people learn something from her act. "Doctors get sick too, and mental illness doesn't discriminate. If you hear my comedy, you hear me, it's my voice. Most of my comedy is based in reality. I mean, I don't really want people to come to my house after the show, but I do still have a suitcase full of Mary Kay products."

Molly has plenty of time to figure out her future, and her mom is confident she will. "I just wish I could get a peek into what the future holds, you know. But I do think it's going to be really good, down the road. That's what I think."

CONCLUSION

You've read our stories ...

- Lorayne is one of the bravest people we know. She has every reason to be bitter and angry, but she sees each day as a new beginning. She inspires us and many others because comedy changed her perspective on life.

- Dave transformed from sadness, to hope and optimism. Now he finds humor in life and shares that humor to make himself laugh and to make you laugh. He can talk to people about his mental illness, share his story, and change how people see others with mental illness. We have lives and personalities and humor, but mostly, we're just regular folks.

- Martin lives with autism and has blossomed in confidence, connecting with his world. We will never forget the look in his eyes when he realized the audience was with him. His dad recently told Dave that we created a smart-ass. Dave said "Yeah, but he's a smart-ass with timing!"

- Tara is no longer victim to the chaos of her nieces' mental illness. Because of comedy, she now has a calling to speak and perform, spreading the word as an outstanding educator and advocate for people with mental illness.

- Eric faces the challenges of life with schizophrenia while making the most of his opportunities. He's taken what he's learned and is helping others, facilitating support groups when he isn't making people laugh.

- Molly was a good doctor until bipolar disorder got in the way and she had to stop doing what she loved. Once afraid she wasn't good at anything, Molly hasn't stopped writing great jokes since she found comedy and our little troupe.

But what about yours?

What about your story? Because we hope this book changes your story, too. We hope that you see people who live with mental illness in a new way, and you share it with others. Share this book, and the stories of these amazing people. Then, share your story, or listen to someone else's. It will make a difference.

What do we hope changes now?

Well, for starters it would be great for us all to begin imagining what it would take to live in the world proposed by SMH founder Dave Granirer, a world in which people could call in sick to work for a mental illness day — a world in which they could call and say their bipolar is acting up and they need extra quiet, or their voices are noisy that day so they are coming in to the office but will be stepping out of a couple of meetings. It would be great to live in a world where managing the symptoms of mental illness was viewed as just another health issue, like managing the symptoms of an arthritis flare, or chronic migraines.

In that world, if a person took some time off or altered their schedule to accommodate those symptoms, when they returned people would simply check in, ask how they're doing, and then move on with their day. No stigma, no big deal, no whispered conversations, and no discrimination.

As for the rest of us, when people have a sick family member, a child in the hospital, a surgery, we've generally got the appropriate societal response down pat: call, send a note, visit, send flowers, bring a casserole, repeat. But when a person is hospitalized or sick with a mental illness, there is far too often complete silence. No calls, no visit, no casserole, no nothing.

That must change. Mental illness can be devastatingly isolating, yet connection to other people is life-changing and life-saving both for those with the disease and for their friends and family. Reach out. Call. Ask if you can help them find resources, or if you can sit with the sick person for a while to give their family members a break. Ask how they're doing, and listen. Don't offer platitudes or clichés, don't feel like you have to be an expert, don't change the subject and for the love of all that is good and holy in this world don't recommend this great diet your uncle tried/fabulous cleanse from Mexico/herbal potion from your backyard/magical incantation to the fairy spirits. Just don't.

What helps? LISTEN. Ask questions, empathize, cry with

them, hug them and tell them you love them, they deserve better and you're not going anywhere. If it's your thing and their thing, pray with them. That's all, and that's enough. Especially if you keep showing up. If they aren't in the mood, respect that, tell them you love them and you'll check in next week.

Don't misunderstand; we're not saying mental illness is no big deal. Hardly. Mental illness is a very big deal, and it often sucks.

Those who live with severe mental illness must have significant resources around them—health care, therapy, support structures. Too often, they don't. We'd like to see that change too, so everyone involved is aware what will be required for a person to heal and recover.

So many tragic news events involving people who live with mental illness might have ended differently if the world in which those things happened was different. What if we all offered a more open, accepting, and supportive embrace for people struggling with mental health and their family and caregivers? What if there was effective medical treatment for mental illness available to all who needed it, and if there was no shame or stigma in reaching out to get that help?

What if we all expected recovery?

In our experience, too many people still believe that a diagnosis of severe mental illness means that's it, finito, the end, period, stop. Life will be irreparably changed for the worse, and a person will always be as sick as they are on their worst day.

Not. True.

Recovery IS possible for many people with even the most severe mental illness, and focusing on the hope of recovery is **critical,** both for the person who is ill and for those around them. Organizations like NAMI offer free classes, free education, and free support that can help people find their way toward recovery. *(Guess what? It's not free for NAMI, so drop them a donation, would ya?)*

Recovery may not look like life before, or the life you had planned, but it is possible. Meaningful, purposeful life is possible, a life with moments of joy and human connection and helping others.

No, Really, We Want You to Laugh

Obviously, we also want you to laugh. We don't care if it's a dainty tee-hee or a big old belly laugh or an ear-piercing cackle. Just laugh. Life can be ridiculous, even in the painful dark moments, and laughter opens us up to the possibility that we can own the ridiculous, instead of it owning us.

Laugh with us, not at us, and you join hands with us in a way that says, "I'm with you, we're together, and that's hysterical!" Laugh with us, and you allow us to share a tiny glimpse into our unique human experiences, a peek into our unique stories. When you laugh with us, you acknowledge us as worthy human beings; you trust us with your own vulnerability in that mysterious moment when you physically and emotionally respond to us with your gift of laughter. In that moment, there is a surprising dignity for us and for you. That moment, that dignity, and that laugh? That's what we all need.

That's no joke, because our hope is to touch many more lives, one joke and one story at a time.

Dave Mowry and Tara Rolstad

LIVING WITH SOMEONE WITH MENTAL ILLNESS

If you know someone who has mental illness, it affects you too. The first and most important thing you can do is help him or her get the right diagnosis and treatment. You may need to make the appointment and go with him or her to see the doctor. Encourage your loved one to stay in treatment. Finally, remember to take of yourself, as being a caregiver can be incredibly stressful and can affect your health as well.

To help a friend or relative, you can:

- Offer emotional support, understanding, patience, and encouragement

- Learn about mental health and mental illness so you can understand what your friend or relative is experiencing

- Talk to your friend or relative and listen carefully

- Listen to feelings your friend or relative expresses and be understanding about situations that may trigger their symptoms

- Invite your friend or relative out for positive distractions, such as walks, outings, and other activities
- Remind your friend or relative that, with time and treatment, he or she can get better.
- Never ignore comments from your friend or relative about harming himself or herself. Always share such comments with close family, their therapist or doctor, or if they're in immediate danger, call a crisis line or 911.

In a Crisis

- If you are thinking about harming yourself, or know someone who is, tell someone who can help immediately.
- Call your doctor.
- Call 911 or go to a hospital emergency room to get immediate help or ask a friend or family member to help you do these things.
- Call the toll-free, 24-hour National Suicide Prevention Lifeline at 1-800-273-TALK (1-800-273-8255); TTY: 1800-799-4TTY (4889); or text HOME to 741741.
- Make sure you or the suicidal person is not left alone.

If you or someone you love is struggling with a mental illness, there are many places you can get educated and get help. We are particularly fond of the National Alliance on Mental Illness (NAMI), which offers great information and classes. Contact your local NAMI chapter at www.nami.org.

ABOUT THE AUTHORS

Dave Mowry

Before comedy, co-author Dave Mowry lived a life of tremendous loss, and years of paralyzing anxiety and depression. The accomplished business owner and CEO lost everything—his companies, his home, and his relationships. The power of laughter transformed Dave's story into one of healing, restoration, and hope. Dave lives near Portland, Oregon with his wife, Heather.

Tara Rolstad

Nothing prepared co-author Tara Rolstad for the shocking surprises she faced as foster mom to a teenage niece with severe mental health issues. Navigating suicide attempts, hospitalizations and lengthy residential treatment stays thrust Tara into trial-by-fire situations not covered in any conventional parenting book. Now as a professional speaker on mental health, comic, and writer she gives voice to the experiences of exhausted family members. Tara lives near Portland, Oregon with her husband David and three boys. You can reach Tara at tara@tararolstad.com.

Made in United States
Troutdale, OR
01/22/2024

17065767R00100